*Anita Carman is brilliant. I am thrilled about her ministry. She has substitute taught for me in Sunday school and at retreats. I trust her teaching totally.*
> —Beth Moore
> Speaker and bestselling
> author of *Get Out of That Pit*

*Anita Carman loves Jesus firsthand and foremost. She has passion for the Lord and a love for God's daughters. God has mixed these two ingredients and given her a ministry of blessing, caring, training, and loving that is infectious. We need more Anitas!*
> —Jill Briscoe
> Bestselling author and speaker

*Anita Carman is a visionary leader who invests in women of all ethnicities. I am so grateful for Anita and Inspire Women's passion to protect the privilege of all women to be established in His Word.*
> —Kay Arthur
> Co-founder—Precept Ministries International

*Anita's love for the Lord, His Word, and His work is not only obvious to everyone but is also contagious. Her passionate relationship with God is like a sweeping fire that causes others to burn with the same spiritual fervor. Prepare to be blessed by Anita and Inspire Women.*
> —Priscilla Shirer
> Speaker and author of *A Jewel in His Crown*

*Anita Carman moves at Spirit-compelled speed with a contagious energy to expand God's kingdom on earth. I commend the marvelous ministry of Inspire Women!*
> —Dr. Tony Evans
> Author, speaker, and
> president of The Urban Alternative

D1056660

*Anita's life, testimony, and communication skills, make her uniquely qualified to impact all those she comes in contact with. Her passion is highly contagious. She truly is a visionary leader crossing generations and ethnicities, bringing a message of hope. Time and consistency prove the character of individuals and organizations. The fruit of Anita Carman and Inspire Women will prove to be of great import and impact to countless lives.*

 —Dr. Doug Stringer
  Founder—Somebody Cares America

*Anita Carman graduated top of her class at Dallas Theological Seminary. We at Dallas Seminary are thrilled to watch how God is using Anita to inspire women across ethnicities to take the study of God's Word seriously and to apply the relevance of His Word to transform lives in families, workplaces, and communities.*

 —Dr. Mark Bailey
  President—Dallas Theological Seminary

# ANITA CARMAN
*with* DANA WILKERSON

# *Transforming*
## FOR A
## PURPOSE

Fulfilling God's Mission as Daughters of the King

MOODY PUBLISHERS
CHICAGO

All Scripture quotations, unless otherwise indicated are taken from the *Holy Bible, New International Version*®. NIV®. Copyright © 1973, 1978, 1984 by International Bible Society. Used by permission of Zondervan. All rights reserved.

Editor: Dana Wilkerson
Interior Design: Ragont Design
Cover Design: Smartt Guys design
Cover Image: iStockPhoto
Author Photo: Alexander-Houston

Library of Congress Cataloging-in-Publication Data
Carman, Anita.
    Transforming for a purpose : fulfilling God's mission as daughters of the King / Anita Carman with Dana Wilkerson.
        p. cm.
    ISBN 978-0-8024-5855-1
    1. Church work with women. 2. Women in church work. 3. Women—Religious life. I. Wilkerson, Dana. II. Title.

BV4445.C37 2009
253.082—dc22

                                                        2009000959

We hope you enjoy this book from Moody Publishers. Our goal is to provide high quality, thought-provoking books and products that connect truth to your real needs and challenges. For more information on other books and products written and produced from a biblical perspective, go to www.moodypublishers.com or write to:

Moody Publishers
820 N. LaSalle Boulevard
Chicago, IL 60610

1 3 5 7 9 10 8 6 4 2

*Printed in the United States of America*

*Dedicated to my husband, Robert Carman*
*who selflessly serves God and his family,*
*my two sons Robbie and Thomas*
*who are their mother's greatest cheerleaders,*
*and my spiritual daughter Mia Yoo*
*whom I can always trust to finish God's mission.*

# CONTENTS

# ACKNOWLEDGMENTS

*T*hose who have journeyed with me in my life and in the ministry of Inspire Women have often heard me say, "The best part of the journey is YOU!" As God broke me to transform me into a vessel for His purpose, how can I find words to say "Thank you" to family and friends who believed in what God was doing in and through me before I saw it?

To my husband, Bob, you are God's most precious grace gift in my life. Thank you for creating a loving and safe environment from which the boys and I could discover our gifts and develop them to potential. To my son Robbie, thank you for all the times you inspired me with your wisdom. While you were still in high school, you were the one who taught me that we don't get to decide if we want to soar as an eagle or if we would rather mingle with the crowd. You reminded me, "God is the one who has chosen!" To my younger son, Thomas, I can still hear you say, "Relax, Mom, no one is perfect but God!" You taught me to lean on God's perfection and not overwhelm myself with the pressure to save the world in my own strength!

To my father, Daddy and Opa, thank you for releasing me to leave our country when it would have been so much easier to keep me by your side. To my brother Bobby and my sister-in-law, Kathy, thank you for remembering Mom's dream and bringing me to the promised land of America. To my sister, Rosita, thank you for loving me unconditionally and carrying my burdens when they were too heavy for me. On this soil of God's great land, His new story for me began.

I will always remember Alice Peacock, my first discussion leader in Bible Study Fellowship, who made sure I was in class every week to discover healing from God's Word. My deepest appreciation to Beth Moore for being the first to affirm my teaching gift, trusting me to teach her Sunday school class and at retreats. Her vision for me set a new course for my life.

To my favorite professors at Dallas Theological Seminary, Dr. Charles Baylis, Dr. Glenn Krieder, and Dr. Ken Hanna, thank you for pouring your wisdom into my life. To the leaders at the College of Biblical Studies, Dr. William Boyd, Dr. Buck Anderson, John Fosdick, and Beverly Lindgren, thank you for believing in my potential for ministry.

I will forever cherish my memory of Doris Morris, Marge Caldwell, Donna Lewis, and Charles Frost, God's saints who taught me about finishing well. How do I find the words to thank Jill Briscoe who was insistent that I not hide my teaching gift?

Judy Horne, you are God's surprise gift in my life. Thank you for being adamant in making sure my teachings were broadcast over the radio. Puddie Pitcock, thank you for giving me no choice and insisting on distributing my writings to the city.

What the public often see is the victory, but only a few see that the warrior was but a child. As God confirmed His calling in my life to write His truths to inspire others to greater worship and service, He sent courageous women to walk beside me. My forever gratitude goes to Carol Byrd, my prayer warrior, who prayed, cried, and loved me through my past into God's plans for me. I will never fathom God's goodness in appointing me lifetime friends in Cathy Wining

Thomas, who made the trip to attend every study I taught; Ann Thetford, who tirelessly edited my keynote messages; and Kim Watson, who was willing to sit on the floor when the room was full, to take copious notes to pass God's truths on to others.

How do I find words to say thank you to Elizabeth Wareing for stretching my faith and leading me by the hand? Thank you, Linda Dunham, for encouraging me by your friendship. I will eternally be grateful to Donna Fujimoto Cole, Cindy Crane Garbs, Joanie Haley, and the Robert and Janice McNair Foundation, and Julie Jordan and Francie Willis whose support compelled me to take the ministry citywide and nationwide. Deborah Clifton and Lisa Brown, thank you for being friends I could trust with my heartaches, and for offering me stability and consistent support as God expanded the ministry. Sister Theola Booker, thank you for teaching me to worship God by living His dreams. Sister Mia Wright and Lezli Busbee, thank you for opening your heart and your church to me. Mary Ann Belin, thank you for being there for me when we lost Marge and making time for me in the midst of your busy schedule.

To the pastors and copastors at the crossroads of my life, the very mention of your name blesses me. Thank you Brother John Bisagno, Gregg Matte, David Self, William Taylor, Leonard Barksdale, Johnnie Lee, Paul Cannings, and Doug Stringer for all the ways you encouraged me.

God in His mercy also surrounded me with strong godly men who protected His plans for me. Thank you, Harvey Houck, for always telling me to "Keep going!" and for being Inspire Women's lifetime spiritual father. Thank you, Robert Carman, Byron Ubernosky, and Rich Majeres, for building the infrastructure for a ministry that reaches thousands of women. Thank you, Dougal Cameron, for giving me a roof over my head when the ministry was homeless. Thank you, William Morris, for teaching me to make disciples. Thank you, Judge

Paul Pressler, for sharing your teaching platform with me. Thank you, Chan Do, for your tireless labor to help me to communicate the vision of Inspire Women. Thank you, Roy Urrego, for spreading my writings via Inspire Women's Web site. Thank you, Martin Gaston, for joining Ginger's passion for Inspire Women and capturing our story on video. Thank you, Steven Alvis, Richard Otwell, Richard Vane, and Chuck Watson, for your key roles in building Inspire Women's headquarters, a permanent beacon of encouragement and spiritual oasis for women called to missions and ministry. Through you, God protected me so I would have time to write as I journeyed as a pioneer on unfamiliar territory.

God, in His grace, surrounded a weak vessel like me with the perfect colaborers to get me to the next milestone of His mission. To the Inspire Women staff who continued with me in spite of the challenges, Myra Davis, Rhonda Niblack, and Mia Yoo . . . you have clearly laid down your personal dreams and proven the purity of your heart to invest in the potential of God's daughters. To my friend, Jaye Martin, thank you for your global vision for Inspire Women to evangelize the world. To Jennifer Lyell, thank you for taking the initiative to visit me in Houston and invite me to be Moody's next author. Dana Wilkerson, thank you for taking the time to connect with my heart and laboring with me as a "midwife" in birthing this book.

All praise and honor and glory go to God and the friends He trusted with His mission. May God's spiritual movement for His daughters illumine the earth as He transforms the hearts of women of all ethnicities, denominations, and economic levels to complete their appointed mission as the daughters of the King of Kings!

# Foreword

*I* was on a flight last month, and the steward was trying to get people's attention as she went through the preflight procedures. I am a million-mile flyer, and the temptation for me is to switch off since I know the drill by heart. I have learned, however, to put my book down and listen as I should, if for no other reason than to be a good example. As she demonstrated the use of the masks in case oxygen was a problem in an emergency, I heard with new ears, "Put your own mask on first before you assist a child."

I thought about that. Everything in me would want to get life-sustaining oxygen to that child sitting next to me. But the application is obvious. If I'm unconscious I can't help my own child or anyone else's. I can't even help myself!

This material that Anita Carman has written (coming from long experience based in the bedrock of the Word of God) helps you as a leader to put on your own mask first. It is life-giving air. It will help you to get the spiritual oxygen that it is going to take to keep you healthy and thinking clearly in a crisis, acting on Scripture and not responding only to your emotions. And this not only in crisis, but in life service to Christ.

I remember hearing some bad news that literally took my breath away. In fact for days I was in such an emotional turmoil I could hardly breathe. I certainly had no breath for words that would comfort and encourage others around me in the same pain I was in. I had to use my will to review the facts. I knew the safety drill I had heard over and over again. Then I began to function as a leader whatever my emotions were doing to me.

As you work through these principles your heart rate should quiet and your faith should be able to "turn your eyes to the hills, from whence comes your help." (paraphrase) Happy studying! Then go out to be the blessing the world is waiting for.

> In His life,
> JILL BRISCOE
> Author, Bible teacher, and
> international women's leader

# My Story

As you read this book, you will read various parts of my life story as illustrations for the various topics that will be covered. Since those stories will be in topical order instead of chronological order, I thought it would be helpful to give you a brief overview of my life and ministry so you can see where those stories fit into the whole.

I was born and raised in Hong Kong, which was under British rule during those days. My family never had much money, and our goal was to someday move to the "Promised Land" of America, where my sister and I could receive an education, get good jobs, and make enough money to support our family. My mother was especially adamant about fulfilling this dream. My half-brother (my mother's son from a previous marriage) was already living in America, and we dreamed of joining him there.

When I was seventeen, my sister and I were preparing to move to the United States to attend college. We were dismayed to discover that although our visas had been approved, our parents' had not. A few months later, I awoke one morning to find that my mother had taken her own life.

Although my mother's suicide devastated me, I clung to the dream that began in her heart, and moved to America. I attended college in Mississippi and completed a four-year sociology degree in two years.

Shortly before I graduated, my father remarried, which threw my world into a tailspin once again. My father was the only "roots" I had left, and while I understood his need for love and companionship, I felt I no longer belonged anywhere. So since my father no longer needed me to take care of him, I decided to go to graduate school in New York.

I received my Master of Business Administration in 1979, and shortly thereafter I worked at a management consulting job in Washington DC. A year later I moved to New Jersey and joined the ranks of Exxon. While there, I begged God to fill my loneliness, and I met the man who is now my husband.

Immediately following our wedding, Bob and I moved to Brussels, Belgium, where he had been transferred for work. It was a very lonely time for me; I was surprised I still felt loneliness when I was married to such a wonderful man. We soon moved back to New Jersey, where I began working for Booz, Allen, and Hamilton, one of the largest management consulting companies in the world.

On the same day I was offered a major promotion at my job, my husband was offered a promotion that demanded a move to Houston, Texas. So in 1985, we moved to Houston because I knew that my long-sought-for promotion didn't satisfy the emptiness I felt on the inside. In 1986, my first son was born, followed by my second son in 1988.

In 1987, I started attending both Bible Study Fellowship and Sunday school. In 1991, my Sunday school teacher, Beth Moore, invited me to substitute teach for her. I served as a leader in her class for seven years. One day, she told me God had called me to be a speaker and that she believed my ministry was beyond what I could do under her umbrella. I was tired of figuring out my own life, so I simply trusted in her guidance. In 1995, I enrolled at Dallas Seminary's Houston campus as my way to prepare to serve God.

My seminary classes were held on the campus of the College of Biblical Studies, the largest multiethnic Bible college in the country. In 1998, the president of the college (who had been my first seminary professor) invited me to join the college's staff as director of Women's Ministry, and I hadn't even given him my résumé. After accepting the position, I eventually rose through the ranks to become vice president of Special Programs and special assistant to the president.

While I was working for the college, God confirmed in my spirit that He wanted a women's conference that reflected the ethnicities in our city. He also showed me that conferences reach thousands, but in order to mobilize women into service, there must be a strong year-round program to search for those God's Spirit stirred in some way and to empower them through training and resources to serve at their God-given potential. In 2001, the first Inspire Women's conference drew nearly three thousand women with an accompanying luncheon that raised $150,000 in scholarship funds.

In May of 2003, the leaders at the college affirmed God's leading for me to cut the umbilical cord to the college, to take Inspire Women with their blessings, and to operate as an independent not-for-profit organization. At the time I left the college, we had no money in the bank, no office space, and one who walked in faith with me on contract that I wasn't sure how I would pay. As I was driving away from the college with tears rolling down my face, I remember looking at the building in my rearview mirror and hearing God say, "Anita, are you more impressed with a building than with Me?" I answered, "Yes I am! Because there is a building there, there is a receptionist, there is an infrastructure. You are a Spirit!" Then God said, "Now you will see what I will do!" That same month God in His grace allowed me to graduate from Dallas Seminary at the top of my class, which gave me the encouragement I needed as I stepped out in faith to establish the ministry of Inspire Women.

By December of 2003, Inspire Women had organized a city-wide conference and luncheon that drew nearly four thousand women. That same month, $100,000 was deposited in the Inspire Women's scholarship fund. By 2006, Inspire Women had invested more than $1 million to inspire and to train women to serve God's purpose, with the beginnings of an endowment that would forever serve as God's trust fund to invest in His daughters who are entrusted with His dreams for ministry and missions. In 2008, Inspire Women established a permanent Inspire Women Headquarters and spiritual oasis as a perpetual beacon of encouragement to inspire the potential in all God's daughters. Oh, the heart of God, who knew the future and carried us from boxes in the backseat of my car to the solid wooded grounds, flowing waters, and beautiful offices in a permanent home base.

The conferences were only the beginning of the work that Inspire Women is doing in the city of Houston. The ministry has added more intensive leadership training and mentoring through Inspire Women's Leadership Institute. From the thousands the ministry reaches, it searches for those called to leadership and funds biblical resources and scholarships for their biblical training in accredited Bible colleges, seminaries, and specialized programs. Women empowered by Inspire Women serve prison inmates; abused women and children; orphans; women in shelters, halfway houses, and transition centers; at-risk youth; and recovering alcoholics, and they shape various other ministries and missions around the world. As a result of the women who have been sent out and the opportunities God has given me to speak at nationwide conferences, the story of Inspire Women is being revealed all over the world. It is a story of staff He called away from corporate careers to live by faith. It is a story of how the faith friends God rallied would not allow personal circumstances or the economy to thwart God's dreams for His daughters. I pray that what God has birthed at Inspire Women will ignite a spiritual women's movement of His daughters empowered for

His service in every major city throughout the country and the world.

You will read the details of many of these events in the pages of this book. As you do, I pray the story of Inspire Women will affirm you as God's daughter and inspire you to let God transform your emotions to fulfill His dreams that will change the world.

# Introduction

When I began my journey to serve God, I was not alone in my enthusiasm. There were others who vowed to travel with me. Yet today, only a handful of those zealous friends remain. Various statistics show that approximately one-third of Christian leaders will abandon their dream before their time on earth is over. Why? Why do so many leave?

As I reflect on my own life and ministry and the many torpedoes that came my way as I was establishing Inspire Women, I see that the biggest challenge I had to overcome was *me*! I allowed my emotions to defeat me in the past, and there were times I couldn't even get out of bed. But that kind of situation can be disastrous for a life and a ministry. Has this happened to you? Have you ever found yourself in a place where you have given up before the battle was won?

Whether God has given you dreams for yourself, a family, a business, a church, a ministry, a nation, or the world, you are a leader in whatever group God has given you to influence. Your emotions can either fuel a passion to keep you on God's eternal timeline or they can shut you down and disperse your focus all over the map. When your heart shatters and you start grasping for straws to feel whole, you will begin to wander from God's purpose. Instead of acting like a sharpened arrow heading toward a target, your heart can become more like fragments that exploded from a land mine. In this state of disarray, it is easy to abandon any dream that had a chance to make an eternal difference. Has God entrusted you with people that He wants you to lead toward goals with lasting significance? If so, then you must learn to fortify your heart as God's keeper of the vision, the one entrusted to fulfill His dreams.

When you step into God's dreams for you, you are not living in friendly—or even neutral—territory. You are entrenched in enemy territory. The devil doesn't care what you do when you are unfocused and not doing anything for God's kingdom. But once you get focused on God's vision and dreams, you show up on Satan's radar and you can almost hear him say to his minions, "Vessel in motion. Engage and destroy." His goal is to put you out of commission.

One way I have seen Satan destroy us is through our emotions. His strategy is simply to get you to shatter on the inside so that one of two things will happen. Either you won't care enough anymore to make a difference in the world, or you will be totally defeated and not care at all. Neither of these scenarios is desirable.

As I began to train leaders, I asked God what I could teach the women that could be of help to their lives and ministries. I sensed Him saying to me, "Teach them the importance of guarding their hearts, and show them how My Word transformed your emotions before you were ready to establish Inspire Women."

In my life, I have discovered that there are three main emotions that God has helped me overcome through His Word: loneliness, rejection, and fear. God, through His power and grace, transformed those emotions in my life into a passionate purpose to accomplish His dreams. Through this process, He shaped me into a suitable vessel for His purpose, and my prayer is that He will do the same for you.

# A Daughter of the King

No matter what family background you come from or how things were and are done in your earthly family, all believers belong to God's royal family. Imagine a family tree—one of those kinds that you made in elementary school that actually looks like a tree, with little boxes to write in the names of the people in your family. This family tree is God's family tree. Imagine your name written in one of the boxes. You are part of a royal family . . . the royal family to end all royal families . . . the family of God Himself. And that family doesn't include just you and God. It includes all of God's children—those you know now and those you know through Scripture. You are on the same family tree as Abraham, Hannah, David, and Mary. What an amazing family we belong to!

So you are a daughter of the King, and as such, your role is to act according to the customs of the royal family. How does a daughter of the King know how to act? She follows the example of others who have gone before her—the great heroes of the faith that we read about in Scripture. Every family has a code of behavior, and our royal family's code can be found in the Bible. Throughout this book, you will be led to look into God's Word to discover how to transform your emotions for God's purpose, using His counsel and the experiences of His people. The Bible is how God has chosen to speak to us and reveal His character and purpose. The way God transforms your emotions is through *practicing* His Word, not just quoting it. My goal through this book is to give you a tangible way to apply God's Word in your life so that you can respond to your own situations in a royal way. You will learn that a life of faith is not a mystical feeling but is the concrete application of God's Word.

In each chapter of this book, you will learn about different situations that you may face that can result in the emotions of loneliness, rejection, or fear. But it is not exhaustive, nor will any of the situations be exactly the same in your life as they are recorded here. So I will let you in on a little secret that I hope will be helpful to you as you learn to transform your emotions. Whenever you experience an emotion because of a challenge or a decision you need to make, do what God has taught me to do:

- Ask yourself, "What am I feeling? What is the emotion I am dealing with?"
- Ask yourself, "Is the level of the emotion I am feeling in proportion to what just happened? If not, what wound did it open from my past to cause me to overreact?"
- Ask yourself, "Is there a teaching in God's Word that parallels the situation I just encountered? Are there verses that speak to the situation that will give me guidance on how to respond?"
- If you cannot find specific verses, then look for biblical examples of someone who dealt with a parallel situation. Since you are to act as a member of God's royal family, ask yourself, "What is the custom of God's royal family and how would God expect me to act?" A tangible way to learn the customs of the royal family is to study the lives of God's faith heroes and how they responded in a similar situation. Then you can imitate the way the faith hero responded.

A life of faith is a concrete way to respond to our situations and emotions based on what God has revealed in His Word. A person who lives by faith is one who intentionally models her behavior after the right choices of the faith heroes in the Bible and trusts that making such a choice is the best choice, no matter what the outcome. The result is a life that is full of conviction and confidence that comes from making choices that are anchored in truths from God's Word and learning from the lives of those who are part of our spiritual heritage.

There have been many times that I have been saved from abandoning God's dream for me by learning from the mistakes and triumphs of people in the Bible. My prayer is that the same will happen for you. Imagine the freedom of finding your compass in an unchanging God and arriving at a place where no human or event can rob you of your purpose. God alone holds our marching orders and we are to fulfill them with royal character and move with dignity and assurance toward our end goal with a commitment to finish all that the Father has sent us to do. We are not hired help, we are daughters of the King, and He wants us to see with His eyes, feel with His heart, and leave this earth changed with His fingerprints.

As you turn each page of this book, I pray that you will be in awe of a great God who works through earthen vessels. If you let Him, He will transform your emotions to empower you with a passionate purpose to fulfill His dreams for you, your family, your business, your church, your ministry, your community, your nation, or the world.

# Section 1

# Transforming Loneliness

## TO FULFILL GOD'S PURPOSE

# Loneliness

THERE IT IS—LONELINESS—sitting all by itself on a page full of words, taking up space, yet disconnected. Do you ever feel like your life is defined by loneliness—sitting all by yourself in a world full of billions of people?

Loneliness. Nobody is immune from it, but nobody has to accept it. Have you ever given in to loneliness? Do you feel like you have missed out on God's purpose for your life because your loneliness defined you? It doesn't have to be that way.

It is essential to learn how to guard your heart from emotions that can topple you. Let God's Word be your protection against loneliness. If you will allow Scripture to be your compass, it will keep you connected to the God who remains faithful and unchangeable no matter what other relationship or situation changes in your life. "Doing God's Word" is what shows the world that we are part of God's royal family—that we are daughters of the King.

We know that we are sealed into God's family tree when we accept the gift of Jesus' death on the cross as the full payment of our sins through His blood. However, what helps us experience our royal identity and connects our hearts to our heritage is how we act as members of that royal family. If you feel lonely or disconnected from your sisters and brothers, perhaps it is because you are acting out of character for one belonging to God's family tree.

As daughters of the King of Kings, we are to exhibit emotions that are in submission to the teaching in God's Word. When we do what God shows us in the Bible—through the role models we have in our royal brothers and sisters—He will protect our hearts and transform our emotions into positive energy so that we can carry out His purposes. By obeying God's Word, we allow ourselves to be molded in His image and connected to a family line of faith warriors.

Throughout these first four chapters, we will be looking at many of the ways loneliness can enter your life—when something is missing, when you feel you're serving alone, when you lose a leader or colaborer, and when God is silent or delays His response. Once we identify the problem areas, we will look in God's Word to see how our faith ancestors handled those same situations. We will discover how members of God's family overcome the emotion of loneliness to fulfill God's purpose and live out His dreams for our lives.

God can take our times of loneliness and turn them into opportunities for greater focus and a closer relationship with Himself—the God who walks with us forever. In John 14:16–17, Jesus said, "And I will ask the Father, and he will give you another Counselor to be with you forever—the Spirit of truth." The word "forever" is such a comforting word when promised by the one who has the power to deliver on His promises, isn't it?

Imagine a future where you fully realize that you are never alone—where loneliness is conquered and God's purposes are fulfilled in your life. Can you see a glimpse of it? Whether you have dreams for yourself, your family, your business, your church, your ministry, your community, your nation, or the world, you can allow God to transform your feelings of loneliness to fuel a greater passion to accomplish great things.

# Chapter 1

## *When*

### SOMETHING
### IS MISSING

"Unless the Lord builds the house,
its builders labor in vain."

Psalm 127:1

*Q*uestions, questions, questions. They float around in our heads constantly. *What will we have for dinner tonight? How will I get this project done by five o'clock? Do I have enough gas to get home?* These are all questions that have tangible answers. At some point in the near future, we will have the answers to them. But what about these questions:

- *What is this constant searching I feel in my heart?*
- *Why do I keep falling in love with the wrong person?*
- *Why did my mother have to die?*
- *Am I on my own . . . again?*
- *Does anyone else feel this way?*

Do any of those questions strike a chord with you? They do with me . . . because I asked them all at different points in my life. I am just like you. Our stories are different, but we have all felt emptiness, loss, grief, and the emotion that accompanies all of these—loneliness. If you are feeling any of those things right now, know that you are not alone, but also know that you don't have to hold on to those emotions.

Often, loneliness is a result of the search for someone or something to complete your life. You feel like something is missing, and you are possibly letting life pass you by while you search for something elusive that seems to vaporize before your very eyes. Or perhaps you think you have already found what will complete you, but you are paralyzed by the fear that you will lose it and be incomplete and lonely again. If you have these thoughts and feelings, you are not alone. Everyone seems to be looking for the perfect mate, the perfect job, or the perfect business or ministry partner. We think, "If only I could find my soul mate [or my dream job or the perfect co-laborer], then my life would be complete."

Pop culture is notorious for propagating this idea when it comes to the realm of love. Movies tell us that there is one special someone who will complete us. So-called reality television shows depict single people trying desperately to find their one true soul mate in a whirlwind of dates and competitions. Listen to virtually any radio station, and you will hear someone crooning that we are not whole by ourselves. The list could go on and on. But the point is that everyone seems to be searching for a tangible person or thing to fulfill them.

If we buy into the idea that there is one person or thing that will complete our lives, the absence or loss of that person or thing can destroy our sense of direction and send our world into a tailspin. The belief that there is someone on this planet who is essential to complete us or to complete our mission in life also puts unrealistic pressure on other people. Put yourself in the other person's shoes. Imagine being expected to fulfill all of *their* dreams, *their* wishes, *their* desires. Initially it might make you feel special, but after a while . . . claustrophobia, disillusionment, and resentment will begin to set in.

So is the whole world searching for the wrong thing? Are we looking for something that isn't possible?

## God Will Fill Our Need

The truth is that there is something deep within us that longs to be connected with someone who feels our heartbeat. The fallacy, however, lies in the belief that this connection is only for our personal fulfillment. Genesis 2:15 tells us, "The Lord God took the man and put him in the garden of Eden to work it and take care of it." This explanation of Adam's mission was quickly followed by God's declaration that, "It is not good for the man to be alone. I will make a helper suitable for him" (Genesis 2:18). There are two things to notice here. First, God defined the mission—it was to fulfill His purpose, not Adam's. And second, God gave Eve to Adam as a "helper suitable for him." God provided the perfect means to fulfill His mission for Adam—and all of mankind.

There is incredible relief in the belief that if there is anyone or anything missing in our lives that will help us complete our God-given mission, God will fill our need. We are not responsible for deciding who or what we need and finding that person or thing according to our timeline. Just as God provided Eve for Adam, He will provide us—His daughters—with what we need. If that person or thing is not currently on the scene, perhaps God is still clarifying our mission for us. Maybe before we know what relationships we need in our lives, we must first know our mission. How can we know who or what will complete God's mission for our lives if we don't know our mission?

If it is God who puts the someone or something into our lives to help us complete His mission, we can also be secure in knowing that if we lose that person or thing, God will send another. He will protect His own mission. When God sends the perfect person for a marriage, a company, a ministry, or a community, that person serves God's greater mission. If something should happen to that person, God is the one who will shape and send the next perfect vessel into our lives to complete the mission or to join us on the next mission. If we lose that dream job, God will provide something else that will better fit His mission for us.

When we lose someone important from our lives through death, relocation, or other reasons, we often feel like we have lost our mission as well. However, could it be that sometimes God allows someone to leave our lives because their part is complete and either the vision is changing or it will take a different kind of person to take the vision higher?

God is unchanging. But often His particular purposes for His children change with time. He reserves the right to reshape the mission because He holds all missions in His hands. He is the *only* sure relationship we have on planet Earth. He alone can make us truly complete. Other people and things don't complete *us*; they help to complete God's mission for us.

In Psalm 144:4, we read, "Man is like a breath; his days are like a fleeting shadow." How do we expect to find stability in a fleeting shadow? In contrast to human flesh, we find in James 1:17 that, "every good and perfect gift is from above, coming down from the Father of the heavenly lights, who does not change like shifting shadows." No matter what mission God shapes or reshapes, the loneliness in our hearts will dissipate when we cling to the unchanging God who will walk with us every day for the rest of our lives.

## Focus on God's Mission

If there was ever a parent or leader who felt alone and longed for the presence of a child or spiritual child that he had raised, it was the apostle Paul. When Paul was sitting in prison, he said in 2 Timothy 4:11, "Only Luke is with me. Get Mark and bring him with you, because he is helpful to me in my ministry." Recall that this was the same Mark who abandoned Paul during his first missionary journey. This was the same Mark whom Paul refused to bring with him on his second missionary journey, which resulted in a rift between Paul and Barnabas. Acts 15:39–40 tells the story: "They had such a sharp disagreement that they parted company. Barnabas took Mark and sailed for Cyprus, but Paul chose Silas and left, commended by the brothers to the grace of the Lord."

The Bible doesn't tell us exactly what hopes Paul had placed in Mark. I know as a parent and as a leader that anytime I take a personal interest in someone younger than me, I realize that I am investing in the future. When my child or spiritual child disagrees with my values or the mission God has entrusted to me, I find part of myself dying on the inside. I discover that I'm disappointed because I have lost a potential successor to continue the family legacy or a business or a ministry's mission. There are times when I feel anger because the person who I poured my time into stopped caring about what I cared about. I sometimes even feel deceived and take their choices personally because I feel like they wasted my time. When they make the choice to leave, their actions speak louder than words. I view them as releasing themselves from their original devotion and commitment to me. How then could I ever trust them or allow them back into my life?

I wonder if there is someone you once invested in who is no longer in your life. Perhaps you parted ways because of a disagreement. Maybe you are secretly still disappointed or angry with a child or a spiritual child who did not share your values. When we put our personal feelings first, we can hold a grudge for a long time. We may even allow the breach to last forever. But when we put God's mission first, we find ourselves letting go of personal offenses. In Paul's case, he did not dwell on Mark's abandonment or the personal disappointment he felt. Over the years, Mark grew in maturity and understanding and got back on the same page with God's mission. In response, Paul welcomed him back with open arms. Moreover, Paul took the initiative to ask for Mark.

Don't miss the words "because he is helpful to me in my ministry." The ministry was Paul's focus. When God's dreams become the reason for our lives, we are more able to repair relationships that benefit God's purpose. Is there someone you need to allow back into your life because they are God's answer to your loneliness and were intended to be part of your future?

God had a mission for Paul, and He also had a mission for Paul's spiritual child, Mark. We don't know all of the details of God's mission for Mark, but we do know that part of his mission was to work by Paul's side and be helpful to him. He was the younger disciple who was the perfect answer to an older disciple who needed someone who could get to him quickly during a time of need.

God has a mission for each of us, as well. If you don't know what God's mission is for you, take time to identify the unique passions and gifts God has put in you, and consider the background and life experiences He has given you. Then look at your uniqueness in light of what needs to be transformed in your family, workplace, or community. Is there a ministry you were set apart to establish? Is there a company you are uniquely qualified to lead or to create? What is your unique background that defines the race God designed for you to run?

We must submit to God's mission. Psalm 127:1 says, "Unless the Lord builds the house, its builders labor in vain." Under God's mission, may you experience freedom and take the initiative to define your relationships.

## Give It Up

When we grasp the idea that God probably won't use just one person throughout our entire lives to help fulfill His mission for us, we can begin to understand that sometimes He wants us to let go of a relationship. This is often incredibly hard to do. If you once believed in the potential of your relationship with someone your heart is connected to, one of the hardest challenges is to accept that you must release that person and move on. (Please do not misunderstand me here—I am not advocating you walk away from a spouse, unless you have biblical grounds. I was referring to relationships at work and in your ministry or community—and even your children—but not marriage. However, if you are contemplating leaving a spouse, consider that in the Old Testament, the Mosaic Law provided for the certificate of divorce as God's way to protect the woman. God's Word provides biblical grounds to dissolve a marriage as His way to protect a woman betrayed by adultery. Ultimately, God is our perfect husband!)

The question you must settle is whether you are more loyal to God or the people in your life. Do you trust His ability to fulfill His mission for your life, or do you rely more on the people you feel He has given you (and perhaps rightly so) to help complete that mission for a time? Do you believe He knows what's best for your ministry or family? Do you trust God's ability to fulfill His mission for the other person's life apart from you?

Let's go back to the Bible for an example from the life of Samuel. God chose Samuel to be a judge over Israel, and he was also the man God appointed to anoint the first king of Israel—Saul. However, Saul was disobedient to the Lord, and subsequently God rejected him as king. In 1 Samuel 16:1 we read, "The Lord said to Samuel, 'How long will you mourn for Saul, since I have rejected him as king over Israel? Fill your horn with oil and be on your way; I am sending you to Jesse of Bethlehem. I have chosen one of his sons to be king.'"

Just as Samuel mourned for Saul, we often agonize over losing a relationship. We don't want to face the regrets or loneliness that might come. And as in the case of Saul, many times the loss of a relationship is due to the other person's disobedience and rejection of God or His mission, which just adds to our agony. However, it is imperative that we follow God's mission and accept His decisions. Imagine what would have happened if Samuel had clung to Saul and not gone to see Jesse. God would have still accomplished His purpose through Jesse's son David, because God's mission can't be thwarted through human decisions, but Samuel wouldn't have been the one to do it.

Whether you are a leader over a family, business, church, ministry, community, or nation, there will be those you have allowed into your heart whom you had high hopes for and whom you perhaps thought would fulfill you and/or your mission. When they continuously reject their calling and God's plans for their lives, you will find yourself in a place where God will require His plans to continue through someone else. Ultimately, we are not called to help another person reach his or her personal dreams. We are called to support God's dreams. When someone refuses to get on the same page with God, they are fighting against God. And God expects us to choose sides; He demands total loyalty.

Sometimes God wants us to release someone or a situation just for a season—not for a lifetime. Consider the relationship between Barnabas and Paul (also known as Saul). After Barnabas opened the door for Paul to be accepted into the apostles' inner circle, Acts 9:29–30 tells us that Paul "talked and debated with the Grecian Jews, but they tried to kill him. When the brothers learned of this, they took him down to Caesarea and sent him off to Tarsus." God allowed a situation where those in authority decided the best thing for the community was for Paul to be sent away.

If you are sitting in a personal Tarsus while your former ministry is continuing—even prospering—without you, do you wonder what could possibly be happening? Paul and Barnabas both likely wondered the same thing. But while Paul was in Tarsus, we know that God was at work creating the perfect situation for Paul's reentry. Acts 11:19–20 tells us, "Now those who had been scattered by the persecution in connection with Stephen traveled as far as Phoenicia, Cyprus and Antioch, telling the message only to Jews. Some of them, however, men from Cyprus and Cyrene, went to Antioch and began to speak to Greeks also, telling them the good news about the Lord Jesus." We then see that as God's Word spread to the Gentiles, He remembered the one who was called to be His instrument to the Gentiles—Paul (see Acts 9:15). Acts 11:25–26 pronounces the end of Paul's season of separation. It reads, "Then Barnabas went to Tarsus to look for Saul. . . ." This story is evidence that even if we must let go of someone, God may bring that person back in due time. If you are in a place where you have to remove someone from your life or ministry, will you trust that when you put God's purpose first, He will work things out in due time?

Sometimes God asks us to give up a positive relationship with someone who is obedient to Him because that is what's necessary at that time. Perhaps you need to release your child to God so that He can better fulfill His dreams for that child. Or maybe you need to release a ministry partner because that person can better serve God in another ministry until the community is ready for his ministry. The reality is that we must follow God first and foremost. This is the scriptural thing to do. In Matthew 22:37–39, Jesus said, "'Love the Lord your God with all your heart and with all your soul and with all your mind.' This is the first and greatest commandment. And the second is like it: 'Love your neighbor as yourself.'" Anytime we love someone or something more than God, we have violated the greatest commandment of God. Loving our neighbor is the *second* greatest commandment. Putting our neighbors ahead of God is not an option—it is disobedience.

Is there someone in your life that God has instructed you to release? How are you feeling about that? Will you let it cause you to fear the loneliness that might ensue? Or will you find your peace in God's mission? Imagine a bird in a birdcage with the door standing wide open, but the bird will not leave because it is afraid to fly alone. But if the bird never leaves the cage, it will never discover God's plans. It will miss out on how the story was meant to end. Are you willing to trust God and to live in His timing and plans?

## How God Reshaped My Dreams

Though I have experienced loneliness at various times in my life, there is one catastrophic event that caused the kind of loneliness that I never would have imagined possible. When I was seventeen years old, my mother committed suicide. Such an event would be devastating for a child of any age. But the depth of my loss was compounded by the fact that my mother's death seemed to equal the death of my purpose— our dream for our lives.

My mother and I shared the dream of leaving Hong Kong for the promised land of America. Our focus was on reaching political freedom and taking hold of opportunities that would help better our lives on this earth. My sister and I had received scholarships to study in America, and our hope was that our entire family would move across the sea. But when my parents were denied visas to enter the United States, my mother took her life. And in my seventeen-year-old mind, she took my dream with her. She had been my partner in this dream. We were supposed to do it together. And then she was gone.

However, through a series of events, circumstances, both wise and unwise choices, and a number of intervening years, I realized that God still had a dream for me. God's dream for me was not dependent on my mother's choices. He redirected my dreams and gave me a passion for helping others reach God's *eternal* kingdom through freedom in Christ. His mission for me was to help countless women make wise choices with their time, energy, and resources during their time on earth so that they could make a difference in eternity. God transformed my tragic circumstances into renewed purpose. That is how God reshapes a mission.

Throughout the years, God has provided the right people at the right time to help carry out this dream. I have had to give up my personal dreams, God has required me to move on from some relationships, other relationships have literally been ripped from me, and the threat of loneliness has often been a huge reality. But through it all, and through the challenges that still lie ahead, I can be sure of this: "Though he slay me, yet will I hope in him" (Job 13:15). In God, I have found protection, healing, recovery, and the passion to live His dreams as a daughter of the King.

# Chapter 2

## *When You*

### FEEL ALONE
### IN GOD'S CALL

"And surely I am with you always,
to the very end of the age."

Matthew 28:20

If you are involved in ministry, there has probably been a point when you felt nobody else heard the words God spoke to you. You felt completely alone in your mission and your calling. You even wondered if you were following God's voice . . . or someone else's. When we feel we are serving alone, it is common to question our calling—to wonder if we heard God rightly. But we mustn't let the questioning create loneliness. We must use it to clarify our mission and keep following God's voice.

There is a difference between physically being alone and feeling as if you're alone even in the midst of other people. But the secret is to focus on God, no matter who is or is not there for you. We must follow His agenda, not ours or anyone else's. I have found God's calling in my life to be a lonely journey because there are times no one understands His calling for me. However, that is no reason to abandon it or to complain about it. Instead, we must simply continue to join God in what He is doing. What I have learned from studying the lives of the faith heroes in my royal family is this: they were sure of what God called them to do and they kept going in the direction of their calling.

## Know the End Goal

God is not going to tell us all at one time the details of how we will accomplish what He has called us to do. But rest assured He will tell us what we need to know, when we need to know it. One thing we do need to know is the end goal, or we won't know whether we've accomplished what we should. Some end goals are general and others are more specific, but we still need to know what mission we are serving. Is it to make disciples? Is it to secure the financial provision for a ministry? Is it to create an infrastructure for God's purpose that will continue long after we are gone? How will we know we have finished?

In studying the faith heroes of the Bible, there is a consistent pattern of these people not necessarily knowing the "hows" of their calling, but still knowing and focusing on the "what." They knew the end goal—they knew what God wanted to accomplish. When you feel the loneliness of your call because others do not hear God's voice, it is essential that *you* cling to God's voice. His voice is all you have to keep you going. In the absence of affirmation from others, His voice becomes your constant companion. Knowing your end goal becomes your compass.

When God called Abraham out of his native land, He didn't tell Abraham the "hows," but God did give Abraham an end goal. Genesis 12:2–3 says, "I will make you into a great nation and I will bless you; I will make your name great, and you will be a blessing. I will bless those who bless you, and whoever curses you I will curse; and all peoples on earth will be blessed through you."

Abraham knew what God wanted to finish, and so he took the first step to walk into God's unfolding story. In Genesis 12:4–5, we read, "So Abram left, as the Lord had told him; and Lot went with him. Abram was seventy-five years old when he set out from Haran. He took his wife Sarai, his nephew Lot, all the possessions they had accumulated and the people they had acquired in Haran, and they set out for the land of Canaan, and they arrived there." Did you see the words "and they arrived there"? Will you know when you have arrived? If you don't know what your end goal is, then you will find yourself here, there, and everywhere while feeling alone and disconnected. God never meant for us to allow circumstances to drive our lives. We were created to subdue the earth, not be subdued by it. In the image of God and by the example of our faith heroes, we must settle the questions, "What is my end goal? Where am I going and when will I know that I have arrived?" Having an end goal keeps us connected to God's plan.

Before Jesus began His public ministry, His end goal was announced. This is His first recorded public address:

> He went to Nazareth, where he had been brought up, and on the Sabbath day he went into the synagogue, as was his custom. And he stood up to read. The scroll of the prophet Isaiah was handed to him. Unrolling it, he found the place where it is written: "The Spirit of the Lord is on me, because he has anointed me to preach good news to the poor. He has sent me to proclaim freedom for the prisoners and recovery of sight for the blind, to release the oppressed, to proclaim the year of the Lord's favor." Then he rolled up the scroll, gave it back to the attendant and sat down. The eyes of everyone in the synagogue were fastened on him,

and he began by saying to them, "Today this scripture is fulfilled in your hearing." (Luke 4:16–21)

Jesus knew what His goal on earth was to be. He also knew that the way He would bring freedom was to die on the cross for the sins of the world. By His death, we would conquer death. By His resurrection, He would give us His power to overcome evil and live victorious lives in spite of our circumstances.

We read in John 19:30, "When he had received the drink, Jesus said, 'It is finished.' With that, he bowed his head and gave up his spirit." Because Jesus knew the reason for His mission, He could say the words, "It is finished." Unless you know what your mission is, you won't be able to assess if you have finished. A life of faith is one where we don't lose track of our mission, no matter how many turns are in the road, no matter how many obstacles are faced, no matter how many people try to stop us, and no matter how alone we feel.

Paul was given an end goal, but God didn't give it directly to him. Instead, God informed Ananias of Paul's mission in Acts 9:15–16: "Go! This man is my chosen instrument to carry my name before the Gentiles and their kings and before the people of Israel. I will show him how much he must suffer for my name." How merciful of God to confirm Paul's calling through another believer. No matter how alone Paul felt as he went into the unknown territory of the Gentiles, he could always remember that Ananias was there at the beginning and heard God's call for him. God informed both of them that Paul's end goal was to reach the Gentiles, and not just the Jews, as was the plan for others of his day. Paul was to bring God's salvation message to the world.

There came a time in Paul's life when he knew he had finished what God had given him to do. In 2 Timothy 4:6–8, Paul says:

For I am already being poured out like a drink offering, and the time has come for my departure. I have fought the good fight, I have finished the race, I have kept the faith. Now there is in store for me the crown of righteousness, which the Lord, the righteous Judge, will award to me on that day—and not only to me, but also to all who have longed for his appearing.

In spite of times when Paul felt alone in his calling, he had the satisfaction of finishing the race. How did he come to this conclusion? I believe his sense of completion was based on three reasons.

First, Paul knew he had finished the race because he had heard God's voice and had followed Him by preaching to the Gentiles. From the moment Paul heard God's voice, he acted on his mission. He did not forget the details of his calling. Second, Paul knew he had finished because once he heard God's voice, he did not waver. He kept his momentum and set his eyes toward the goal of reaching the Gentiles through every door that was open to him. He tells us in Acts 20:19–21, "I served the Lord with great humility and with tears, although I was severely tested by the plots of the Jews. You know that I have not hesitated to preach anything that would be helpful to you but have taught you publicly and from house to house. I have declared to both Jews and Greeks that they must turn to God in repentance and have faith in our Lord Jesus." And third, Paul was sure he had finished because he anticipated that he was getting close to the end of his time on earth.

Abraham, Jesus, and Paul clung to God's voice and made the end goal their compass in spite of the fact that they were set apart and experienced the aloneness of being trusted with a God-sized mission. This is the custom of God's royal family, and as part of that family, when God speaks to us—His daughters—we too need to grab onto His voice. The longer we wait to obey God's calling, the longer we keep ourselves in a state of loneliness and the more we operate where our hearts are disconnected from their source of true life. It is when we step out in obedience that our hearts will beat as one with God's.

There will be times when you will wish God would just lay out a five-year plan for your life, work, or ministry. But God does not want us to worship a plan or a program. God wants us to discover that He Himself is our plan. When we cling to the resurrected Christ as the living relationship in our lives, He becomes our source of life and daily direction.

Jesus wants us to trust His person as our plan. First we must hear His call as Matthew 28:19–20 says: "Therefore go and make disciples of all nations, baptizing them in the name of the Father and of the Son and of the Holy Spirit, and teaching them to obey everything I have commanded you. And surely I am with you always, to the very end of the age." Next, we must ask if His call is more specific than the general call to help advance His message on earth. Once we settle on the specificity of the call for our lives, we then follow Him through any open doors and opportunities that will put us further along toward the end goal He has given us.

## Be Prepared to Move

God's end goal for our lives often requires us to leave the comfort zone of familiar territory. Change is not uncommon, and change—especially if it means a change of location—often leads to feelings of loneliness. However, God will not be held hostage to our emotional baggage. As members of God's royal family—daughters of the King—He expects us to fit our lives into the family's schedule and His plans for the entire world.

Is God growing you into a woman He can trust with His mission? If so, manage your expectations and learn from God's biblical patterns. Every family has its culture—its ways of doing things. In God's family, the Father is urgent. He will not blink an eye before sending you where He needs you to go. Our family mandate is to take God's message of salvation from where we live to the ends of the earth. So if your company is expanding internationally, don't be surprised if you're asked to go. If your church is starting a church plant in another part of the city, state, or nation, you may be called to be a part of that team. If God allowed a natural disaster to destroy your home, consider that relocating you may be His way of taking His Word in you on the road.

We mustn't cling to our tangible assets too tightly. God will not bless a decision where one of His children declines a calling because of her reluctance to move and sell a house. In fact, it may be that God sees our possessions, well-decorated dream homes, and even the satisfaction we feel from putting down roots as encumbrances. Unless it serves the interest of your royal family for you to live in a palace on earth or to put down roots in a comfortable place, be prepared to leave it all behind to follow God's call at a moment's notice.

This applies not only to young people, but to older ones as well. In the first book of the Bible we read, "So Abram left, as the Lord had told him; and Lot went with him. Abram was seventy-five years old when he set out from Haran" (Genesis 12:4). He was *seventy-five years old*! God didn't seem to be concerned that Abraham was of an age where he might personally prefer to slow down and to surround himself with what was familiar. The very words, "So Abram left" carry with them a sense of loneliness. No matter who we bring with us, just the fact that we "left" implies there were things and relationships we had to release. From our culture's point of view, we might think of a seventy-five-year-old as someone who deserves to retire after a lifetime of working in a place where he feels at home. But if we check God's Word, we will find that there is no biblical example of anyone who retired! Moreover, God does not apologize for commanding us to uproot and to spread His image on this earth.

Interestingly enough, it is usually when we think we have created a place of stability on earth that God stirs in our spirit to begin a new dream. If you have attained a level of financial security, you may think you can just sail away into the sunset for the rest of your life. Instead, it may be that God has strategically positioned you to finish something major that He has planned. I cannot predict what that might be, but it may include leaving your home. The fact is that every new dream is often accompanied with the loneliness of a pioneer who has to lay down new tracks.

The best example of being willing to leave one home for another for the sake of the call can be found in the life of Jesus. Philippians 2:3–8 tells us:

> Do nothing out of selfish ambition or vain conceit, but in humility consider others better than yourselves. Each of you should look not only to your own interests, but also to the interests of others. Your attitude should be the same as that of Christ Jesus: Who, being in very nature God, did not consider equality with God something to be grasped, but made himself nothing, taking the very nature of a servant, being made in human likeness. And being found in appearance as a man, he humbled himself and became obedient to death—even death on a cross!

Jesus left a perfect environment in heaven to come and live here on earth among sinners. In order to accomplish God's mission, He had to move. But notice that the details of Christ leaving heaven to come to earth to die for our sins came following the admonition to "do nothing out of selfish ambition." He also "did not consider equality with God something to be grasped." If we put those two thoughts together, God's perfect counsel instructs us that when we are unwilling to let go of the familiar or when we demand comfort as an equality or right when God's mission demands sacrifice, then we are acting out of "selfish ambition." It's hard to grasp the idea that retiring, refusing to move, or expecting luxuries after years of labor is selfish *or* ambitious, but if it goes against God's desires, it is. Have you traded your royal family's mission for your own personal agenda? Do you ever think, "I deserve this. I worked for this. I paid for this. This is mine and I'm not letting go of it!"? The truth of the matter is that when you chase a personal agenda, you are going against the tide of God's movement on earth. And when you go in the opposite direction of where God is going, you disconnect yourself from God's heart and are walking into greater loneliness.

When God asks you to leave the familiar to enter uncharted territory, instead of dreading or resenting it, receive it as a confirmation that you are in God's royal family—that you are His daughter and as such are privileged to be able to move where He moves. We mustn't forget who our Father is, or we will find ourselves disconnected from His purpose. We serve a Father whose eyes are on the world. He has a mission He wants to complete before the curtain falls on this planet. Earth is temporary, and our real home is in heaven.

## The Battle Is the Lord's

When we listen to God and follow His voice, we need to be aware that we are entering the battlefield. Satan will shoot many arrows at us to try to keep us from accomplishing God's mission. And one of the arrows that most often hits its mark is the feeling of loneliness in our mission.

Do you ever feel sorry for yourself because you think you're all alone? Are you sometimes tempted to give up because you feel no one is fighting beside you? Then consider some of the heroes in your royal family tree.

If asked to name a "loner" in the Bible, who would you pick? Did John the Baptist come to mind? He was a "voice of one" (Matthew 3:3). He lived in the desert and preached to whoever would come. There were times that he was physically alone, and other times when he was surrounded by crowds. Yet he was still a "voice of one." He had a new message to bring in order to pave the way for the Messiah. John's calling was unique. Do you ever feel like you have been called by God to pave the way for something new? Do you feel like you are alone in the desert like John?

Another hero of the faith also found himself alone— Elijah. First Kings 18:22 records Elijah as saying, "I am the only one of the Lord's prophets left, but Baal has four hundred and fifty prophets." He was outnumbered 450 to one. Those are pretty bad odds. But God is in the business of beating the odds. In spite of his aloneness, God enabled Elijah to call down fire from heaven to prove the power of God in front of those very prophets.

When we feel like we are serving alone, we need to remember that God is our commander in chief, and that the battle belongs to Him. Satan often tries to deceive us into thinking that no one is aware of or cares about our mission or the battles we are fighting. He wants us to believe that we cannot make it on our own. We can get overwhelmed when we start to think that we are the one to save the day. But the truth is that the battle is not really ours to fight. As David faced down Goliath, he said, "All those gathered here will know that it is not by sword or spear that the Lord saves; for the battle is the Lord's, and he will give all of you into our hands" (1 Samuel 17:47).

The fact that the battle belongs to the Lord does not mean, however, that we should just sit around and let Him do all the work. It means that we should step out in faith and pour out our lives in service to Him. Whether we are alone or surrounded by colaborers doesn't matter. Knowing that God will win the battles leaves us free to serve without the stress of feeling as if the weight of the world is resting on our shoulders.

The next time you feel the pressure to save the world,

stop and picture the following image of Jesus as described in Revelation 19:11–16:

I saw heaven standing open and there before me was a white horse, whose rider is called Faithful and True. With justice he judges and makes war. His eyes are like blazing fire, and on his head are many crowns. He has a name written on him that no one knows but he himself. He is dressed in a robe dipped in blood, and his name is the Word of God. The armies of heaven were following him, riding on white horses and dressed in fine linen, white and clean. Out of his mouth comes a sharp sword with which to strike down the nations. "He will rule them with an iron scepter." He treads the winepress of the fury of the wrath of God Almighty. On his robe and on his thigh he has this name written: KING OF KINGS AND LORD OF LORDS.

Jesus is the hero who will save the day. When we try to rob Jesus of center stage by taking the credit for ourselves, we will find ourselves feeling overwhelmed over time. The human flesh was never created for greatness. It was created for servanthood. Like John the Baptist, may we serve to point others to Jesus, but may we also serve knowing that the stage belongs to Him. We were designed to decrease so He will increase. John the Baptist said it so well in John 3:29–30, "The friend who attends the bridegroom waits and listens for him, and is full of joy when he hears the bridegroom's voice. That joy is mine, and it is now complete. He must become greater; I must become less."

Instead of laying your gift on the altar and giving God the limelight, do you find yourself trying to keep or gain a title or position or trying to top yourself in performance? If so, you will get irritated when you don't make the goals. And then you will complain that you have no one to help you and that you are all alone. We need to realize that the more God trusts us with success, the more we can get ourselves in a place where we are our own worst enemies. John the Baptist was a "voice of one" crying in the wilderness, but Scripture never tells us that he was overwhelmed by his mission. He didn't lose focus on his purpose and calling. He was not trying to impress anyone. His role was to make a way for the crowds to see Jesus and to get out of the way so Jesus could have the limelight. Our focus on our mission is what keeps our hearts beating as one with God's.

## How God Is Leading Me to My End Goal

As you know, God called me to found Inspire Women. There were other avenues for ministry that could have matched my gifts, but God chose the one that would enable me to inspire women from all ethnicities and denominations and economic levels to connect their lives with His purpose. While this was not anything I would have chosen for myself, I now see that it is my best opportunity to reach the most people for God's kingdom. It also made sense, considering my background. I have found that the dreams God gives us are often connected to the story God has been writing in our lives over the years. It is in allowing God to match my unique background to a need He is meeting in the community that I find my perfect fit in God's plans on earth.

Before walking through the door toward Inspire Women, however, I asked these questions: "God, where does this door lead? What is our destination? When will I know we have finished?" He said He wanted a perpetual infrastructure that will inspire His daughters and provide the funds and opportunity for their training for missions and ministry. God told me He wanted a trust fund to perpetually send the message to the world that He affirms the potential of His daughters for His mission and will invest in their training. He said He had chosen the empowering of His daughters as His way to complete His spiritual army. And not only does He want to do this through His daughters, but He will use both young and old. He will call out the older generation and give them His dreams. Acts 2:17–18 reads, "In the last days, God says, I will pour out my Spirit on all people. Your sons and daughters will prophesy, your young men will see visions, your old men will dream dreams. Even on my servants, both men and women, I will pour out my Spirit in those days, and they will prophesy."

God chose to begin His vision for the financial provision of His daughters across ethnicities and denominations in Houston, Texas. I know I will have finished when the city of Houston has a basic level of funding for women for biblical training. I know I will have finished when the ministry has an annual process to reach thousands with a way to find and to invest in those called to serve in missions and ministry. I also know that God wants this vision to travel to other cities throughout the earth so that His daughters can be mobilized to change the world. I don't know if I will live to witness the vision implemented in other cities, but I know there will come a day when the vision will be completed.

Although I know what the end goal is, I don't know how God will implement His vision. So I go to Him and ask for the plan. In His voice, I will not be alone in my calling. I wake up each morning expecting that He truly does give us each day our daily bread. My security is in Jesus. When Jesus said the Son of Man did not have a place to rest His head (Matthew 8:20), this was an invitation to greater freedom. I have found how little I actually need in terms of my environment in order to succeed. If God gives us a building to operate from, then praise Him. If He gives us a tent, then praise Him. I have found that the treasure is Him.

Today Jesus is seated permanently at the right hand of the Father. The season of having no place to lay His head is over. Could it be that once we make God our only treasure, He transports us into blessings beyond our imagination? Recently, God transported Inspire Women from living in donated office space to having a permanent headquarters and spiritual oasis. From this home base, God will inspire His daughters across the world.

When the Inspire Women's office is full today with the King's daughters streaming down the halls, I marvel at the contrast to the days I sat alone, crying my heart out because there was not one daughter in sight. When the scholarship recipients come to orientation to open their scholarship award letters, I feel God's heart rejoicing.

God continues to astound me. His fingerprints are all over Inspire Women. He moves out of His heart of mercy for His daughters and His global personnel plan to recruit and to send His spiritual warriors with His message to the ends of the earth. One day, no daughter will be left behind. Those who do not currently have the opportunity to be trained for missions and ministry will have the chance to be equipped. Oh how sad it is to think that we would be sending our military out to battle without ammunition! In the same way, God wants His daughters to be fully equipped before He sends them to intervene in the battles of life.

I still am not quite sure how I ended up as the founder and president of Inspire Women. Did I ever want to start my own 501(c)3 nonprofit ministry? Never in a million years! But God did not ask me what I wanted. What has surprised me is how over time, I discovered that doing what God wanted fulfilled the desire of my heart.

God was sure of His plan, but I discovered it moment by moment by walking through the next open door that aligned with His vision. When God told me to flow with Him, I discovered how insecure that made me feel because I didn't know Him. I knew Him with head knowledge, but I had to get out of the boat before I could experience walking on water with Jesus. God, in His mercy, held on to my hands one day at a time and allowed me to witness His faithfulness. During the times I felt I was all alone, He reminded me that the battle is His. Where I failed, He covered me with His grace.

Even though we are fallen creatures, God has chosen to work through His daughters whom He trusts with His mission. Are you one of God's daughters? Then I pray you will become a part of God's victory story and fulfill the dreams He puts in your heart to complete His vision to save the world.

# Chapter 3

## *When You*

### LOSE A LEADER
### OR COLABORER

"God sets the lonely in families."

Psalm 68:6

Have you ever been in a situation where God called you out from a church or a workplace, or out from under a specific authority figure in your life? Did that leave you feeling alone? Did it leave you feeling like you were drifting?

There have been several times in my life when following God's call meant leaving a leader I relied on, counted on, leaned on. After one of those times I immediately latched onto another leader, trying to hide under her wings. Because I hadn't envisioned myself as a leader at that point, I operated like a Timothy searching for the great apostle Paul that I could follow. I didn't realize that God had placed me under that previous leader for a season, and then He wanted me to go out into the world as His royal ambassador.

Although at one point in my life, God put teachers around me to lead me to Him, He didn't want me to stay there. Instead, He used those leaders to help transition me into becoming a leader who would hear

His heart for myself. Gone were the days when I could live off someone else's adventure with God. He wanted me to enter into an adventure of my own with Him. Is He wanting you to do the same? Is He changing your relationships to bring you to a place where you can be a stronger leader for Him?

## God Is Good

When a pastor or worship leader says, "God is good," what does the congregation immediately say back? You got it: "All the time." And then we even say it the other way around just for good measure. "All the time ... God is good." This ritual can be heard in churches all over the country on a Sunday morning. The question is: Is it just a ritual, or do we really believe it? Do we really and truly believe that God is good all the time?

Our ability (or inability) to flow with the changes in our lives comes from our belief (or unbelief) in the goodness of the Change Agent Himself. Romans 8:28 tells us that "in all things God works for the good of those who love him, who have been called according to his purpose." This verse gets bandied about in all kinds of situations, but it's often hard to believe the truth of it. But the fact of the matter is that if we are truly confident of God's goodness, we will be able to trust the changes God allows in our lives. We will trust that God will work things out "for the good" because we understand and acknowledge that goodness is His very nature.

Let's take a look at the next part of the verse: "of those who love him, who have been called ..." That's us—the daughters of the King. God loves us, calls us, and works for the good of His daughters and sons. This verse also tells us that the good God works out in the lives of those He has called will be "according to his purpose." When you don't understand the changes in your life, you can rest in saying and believing, "But I know God is good, and I know that whatever He has allowed to happen is an expression of His goodness to fulfill one of the reasons He has called me." If God is changing your relationships, you can believe that He has good reasons for it.

In order to accurately assess what is good in life, you must first be in tune with what God has called you to. For example, if you are called to display God's power through a loss, then praising God for the loss will create the stage for you to reveal His power—and that is a good thing, is it not? When the changes in your life don't make sense, try asking the questions, "What statement is God making through my life? How will those changes in my life help fulfill my calling?" Connecting your situation with the purpose to which you were called will show you how God is working things out for your good.

Do you believe that God is good through *all* of the circumstances of our lives? Consider this example. There was a preacher who invited his congregation to repeat the words, "God is good," after each statement he made. He said, "I got a promotion," and the response was, "God is good." The preacher said, "I got married," and the congregation responded, "God is good." "I had a baby," was followed by, "God is good." Then the preacher said, "My wife left me for another man." Everyone in the room hesitated, and then some reluctantly said, "God is good." Finally, the preacher stated, "My baby died." No one said, "God is good."

This preacher was making the point that we don't really trust God's goodness. In fact, we are constantly assessing God and evaluating His goodness. But imagine how different our lives would be if we settled the question of God's goodness once and for all. Can you believe with all your heart that God is good and that He will work things out for good no matter what is happening in your life?

## God Sets the Lonely in Families

It can be hard when God removes someone from our ministries or lives—whether a leader, a colaborer, or even a family member. In the past, when God led me from under the umbrella of leaders I have been privileged to serve, I did not understand. Why would God remove these people who I would have gladly served with forever? In hindsight, I realize that God was not trying to take someone from me, but instead He was trying to give me so much more. It was the loss of those relationships that left me free to build the ministry that God had called me to. He led me to new relationships and a new "family."

We need to trust God to assign new people to our lives instead of demanding that our lives be reserved for certain individuals. He will take care of us according to His purposes. The King will provide for His daughters. Psalm 68:4–6 says, "Sing to God, sing praise to his name, extol him who rides on the clouds—his name is the Lord—and rejoice before him. A father to the fatherless, a defender of widows, is God in his holy dwelling. God sets the lonely in families, he leads forth the prisoners with singing; but the rebellious live in a sun-scorched land."

It is God who sets the lonely in families, not us. He chooses who will be in our lives, who will lead us, who we will lead, and who will walk alongside of us. We see an example of this in Jesus' life. Even as He was hanging on the cross, He took the time to let His mother know that she would not be alone. "When Jesus saw his mother there, and the disciple whom he loved standing nearby, he said to his mother, 'Dear woman, here is your son,' and to the disciple, 'Here is your mother.' From that time on, this disciple took her into his home" (John 19:26–27).

We also notice from the Psalm 68 passage above that "the rebellious live in a sun-scorched land." In your life, have you resisted or rebelled against the new relationships God has put in your path to replace the ones He has removed? If so, consider God's goodness. Know that He is working for your good according to His purposes. He is the King, and you are His daughter, and He will not lead you astray.

Will you trust God's decision and submit to the way He chooses to "set the lonely in families"? Don't live in a sun-scorched land. It's time to let go of our loneliness by accepting God's goodness, His plan for us, and the dreams He has given us.

## God Is Our Dream Maker

Losing someone who is important to our life and ministry can sometimes make us feel as if our dream has died—as if our calling can no longer be fulfilled. But the truth is that God's dreams for us do not rest with other human vessels. Colossians 1:16–17 says, "For by him all things were created: things in heaven and on earth, visible and invisible, whether thrones or powers or rulers or authorities; all things were created by him and for him. He is before all things, and in him all things hold together." Did you notice what that said? We were created *by* God and *for* God. We weren't created to fulfill each other's dreams. We were created to fulfill God's dreams. God is our dream maker, and it is up to Him—not us or anyone else —to make sure the dream is fulfilled. Consider who you would rather have fulfill your dream—the all-powerful Creator of the universe or a sinful human. Looking at it from that standpoint, the choice is clear, isn't it?

Let's take a look at how some of the members of our royal family tree handled losing relationships. When Jesus was on earth, there were three men that He drew close to more than the others—Peter, James, and John. They got to go places with Him and share things with Him that no one else did. Matthew 17:1–2 tells us, "Jesus took with him Peter, James and John the brother of James, and led them up a high mountain by themselves. There he was transfigured before them. His face shone like the sun, and his clothes became as white as the light." They alone were with Jesus when He raised Jairus' daughter from the dead. "He did not let anyone follow him except Peter, James and John the brother of James" (Mark 5:37). They shared the most intimate moments of Jesus' agony at Gethsemane. "He took Peter, James and John along with him, and he began to be deeply distressed and troubled" (Mark 14:33).

And then they lost Him—Jesus, their leader, their rock, their compass. He was gone. Not too long after that, they also lost one of their own. "It was about this time that King Herod arrested some who belonged to the church, intending to persecute them. He had James, the brother of John, put to death with the sword" (Acts 12:1–2). The loss of a leader and a co-laborer so close together could have signaled the end of Peter and John's ministries. They would have been justified in giving up the dream, right? Wrong. Instead, they focused on God's dreams for the world.

## God's Mission on Earth

Let's take a small peek into my diary at a time when I was facing the loss of a leader that I very much admired. On January 15, 1998, I wrote:

> I am learning facts about You I never knew. More than that, You are no longer a fact, but a Person with a history and dreams for the future. I am beginning to understand that this world isn't about my story; it's about Yours. Before now, it never occurred to me that You have plans for this time and age, and that I exist to fulfill Your plans. The strangest thing has happened. My relationships with others don't feel so urgent anymore. What is essential is my relationship with You.

We find our stability in God's mission on earth. When everything changes, the one constant we can count on is the unchanging heart and mission of God. All authority has been given to Jesus. With that authority, He commanded us to "go and make disciples of all nations . . ." (Matthew 28:19–20). God has sounded His clarion call and He will not stop until every knee will bow "and every tongue confess that Jesus Christ is Lord" (Philippians 2:10–11). Jesus said in John 5:17, "My Father is always at his work to this very day, and I, too, am working." My question to you is, "Are you working with Him?"

## How God Released Me from Influential Leaders

I would be remiss in encouraging you to boldly work with God through changing relationships if I didn't give you some tangible examples from my own life. The following story is not meant to show you how faithful I am, but to show you how faithful God is when we submit to His plan and purposes for our lives and His kingdom.

In January of 1987, I attended Sunday school for the first time. You'll never guess who taught that class. Beth Moore. Yes, *that* Beth Moore. As I began to sit under her teaching, I felt my heart begin to heal from the many wounds of my past. God used Beth and her ministry to women to help bring me out of emotional bondage.

After a while, I began to serve under Beth's leadership. I ministered as a leader in Beth's class for seven years. She would call me to substitute teach when she was out of town, and she invited me to speak at retreats. I thought my calling was to be the best substitute teacher she ever had. I wanted her to trust me to go anywhere to teach God's Word and not worry about what I might do or say.

Then, one day, Beth told me that God had spoken to her heart and He told her that my ministry would extend beyond the covering of her umbrella. She did not know where God was taking me but she encouraged me to follow His voice.

When God released me from Beth's class, I felt like a duck

out of water. I had found my security in hiding under Beth's wings. I kept trying to run back to where I felt safe. One of those times, Beth said to me, "Anita, I feel like you think you need something from me, but you don't need anything from me. You have the cloak. Just dip it in the water." She was comparing our relationship to that of Elijah and Elisha. Elisha didn't want to be separated from Elijah any more than I wanted to be separated from Beth. However, just as Elisha needed to spread his wings and fly without Elijah, I also needed to step out in faith and trust in God—not in my earthly relationships —to lead, encourage, and guide me.

So in 1995, I enrolled at Dallas Seminary's Houston campus in order to better prepare for God's service. During my first semester there, I met the next leader who had a great impact on my life—Dr. William Boyd. Dr. Boyd was one of my professors, and he was also the president of the College of Biblical Studies in Houston. A few years after starting seminary, Dr. Boyd offered me a job at the college as the Director of Women's Ministry. He said when he was praying about who to hire for this new position, my homework fell out of his files. Unbeknownst to me, he had been passing out my homework to his students as an example of a perfect research paper. Seeing my paper brought me to his mind for the position. He offered me the job, and I accepted.

During my time at the college, Dr. Boyd kept trusting me with more responsibilities until I became his special assistant and the Vice President of Special Programs at the largest multiethnic Bible college in the country. A series of encounters with the students led me to begin raising scholarship money for women who could not otherwise continue with their studies. At the time, I didn't realize that God was using those encounters to stir a passion in my heart to ignite a spiritual women's movement to inspire and empower all God's daughters to change the world with the power of His Word in action.

In 2001, the leaders of the college decided they wanted to hold a citywide women's conference, and I was tagged to plan and implement the conference. This first conference drew nearly 3,000 women from more than 650 churches! Two years later, the College of Biblical Studies made the decision to focus on a building campaign and to redirect my time to support other programs instead of the Inspire Women Conference. When I explained my passion was with women's ministry, Dr. Boyd chose to affirm my potential and gave me his blessing to leave the college and to take Inspire Women with me and do with it as God led. He wrote a beautiful farewell letter to friends of the college saying he felt like a father releasing his daughter to work in a different vineyard.

I dreaded the idea of leaving the college after five years of service there. I had mentored many women during that time—my spiritual daughters—and had put down roots again. God was asking me to leave a leader, just as He had done a few years earlier. But I knew that Inspire Women had the potential to reach many women who couldn't be reached when it was running within the confines of the college. I knew that if I stayed with the college, I would never discover all of the amazing places God could take Inspire Women. I would always think about "what could have been." Something inside me felt that Inspire Women had the potential to become a great engine to find God's gems in the city of Houston and to train women in the programs that best fit their calling. I realized that those programs should not be limited to the training offered by one college. I believed that what God was doing for the women in Houston would one day be replicated in every major city throughout the country. The only thing standing between me and God's vision was . . . me. Would I walk away from what was tangible and visible—leaders and colaborers that I knew and loved and trusted—and believe in the vision God had entrusted to me?

I did walk away from the people and the institution that

had meant so much to me—that had contributed so much to my spiritual growth. And oh how God has blessed that decision. It hasn't always been easy. But I do know that if I had stuck with Dr. Boyd—the leader God wanted me to release myself from—there would be no Inspire Women. I don't even want to think about what I would have missed out on—and what the thousands of women who have been touched by the ministry would have missed out on. Likewise, if I had never left the covering of Beth Moore's wings, I would not have had the experiences at the College of Biblical Studies that prepared me for leadership in Inspire Women. Do you see the cycle here?

I will be eternally grateful for Beth, Dr. Boyd, and the other leaders God has placed in my life through the years. They have taught me much, and my life and ministry wouldn't be the same without their influence. But I believe that when God releases us from a leader, it is because He has finished what He wanted us to learn under that leader and because He wants us to step into His new vision for our lives. He doesn't want us to live in our past relationships, but to embrace the new relationships He gives us to accomplish His purposes in the world.

# Chapter 4

## When God

### IS SILENT
### OR DELAYS

"But my righteous one will
live by faith"

Hebrews 10:38

God's delays have often perplexed me. It seems to me that since His goal is to reach the world for Him, then when I ask Him, "What do You want me to do with my life?" He should answer quickly and immediately so I can get on with whatever it is He wants me to do. Instead, there is often silence. But why would God be silent if He desires me to do His will?

I wonder how many people have said to God, "I surrender all," and, "Wherever You lead I'll go," and honestly believed they meant it, but then have been left standing there with no further direction. That has happened to me, and so I have often felt very alone while waiting for God to speak. I kept thinking the problem was God, but one day God opened my eyes to see that the problem was *me*.

I realized that God often was waiting to answer because I was not ready. I "surrendered all" without understanding the cost. I said I would go wherever He led, but my willingness to go was really based on my own ideas about where I was going. My intention wasn't for God to tell me what He wanted me to do, but for Him to bless *my* plans. It hadn't occurred to me that God had plans of His own and that I existed for His purpose. To my total shock, I realized that God was silent because He was showing grace. He was silent because I was still in preparation for the call. He knew I wasn't ready.

We know that God is the perfect steward of His resources—and those resources include us. He doesn't waste our gifts and talents, but He might wait to use them until we are perfectly prepared for the task He has for us. So if God hasn't spoken, it must be because it's not time. He is still in preparation, and we are part of that preparation.

It took years for God to prepare me to launch Inspire Women. As I look back at my life, I see how His delay was for my preparation. I was in Bible Study Fellowship for six years, in Beth Moore's Sunday school class for seven years, and at Dallas Theological Seminary for seven years. Although I felt restless through much of that time—wanting to get on with it and *do* something—I was not ready yet. The ministry required major sacrifices from my family and me. It required a reprioritization of our time, energy, and resources. In any great work God plans on doing, He takes the time to prepare His daughters for what He has called them to do.

Times of silence can often be equated with delays. God delays answers to our prayers until we are ready—thus, the silence. What should we do during those delays? One thing we can do is never stop trusting Him. Another thing we can do is to assess whether or not we truly understand and are ready to accept His calling for us. His silence may be because He is waiting for us to answer Him, not the other way around.

# Understanding the Calling

God orchestrates the events of our lives to lead us to His calling for us. But still so many of us miss the boat or shrink back from what He wants us to do. He leads us to what He wants, and then He waits for us to understand and accept it. Through my own experiences, God has shown me that there are three stages to understanding and accepting our calling.

The first stage is simply to declare that you will follow Him. The second stage is to fully appreciate the cost and be willing to pay it. And the third is to acknowledge that the only way you can give God what He desires is through leaning on Him and trusting in His power. Let's take a look at each of these stages in more depth.

## Declare That You Will Follow

This stage may sound obvious. After all, if we don't plan to follow God's call, why would we want to understand it? However, it is not as easy as it might seem. When initially confronted with God's plan, we may feel overwhelmed and immediately shrink back from it. We might not want to respond for various reasons.

Luke 9:57–62 tells of several situations where those who professed their desire to follow Jesus immediately came up with all kinds of reasons to justify delaying their obedience (which, in fact, is disobedience).

> As they were walking along the road, a man said to him, "I will follow you wherever you go." Jesus replied, "Foxes have holes and birds of the air have nests, but the Son of Man has no place to lay his head." He said to another man, "Follow me." But the man replied, "Lord, first let me go and bury my father." Jesus said to him, "Let the dead bury their own dead, but you go and proclaim the kingdom of God."

Still another said, "I will follow you, Lord; but first let me go back and say good-by to my family." Jesus replied, "No one who puts his hand to the plow and looks back is fit for service in the kingdom of God."

God wants us to respond to Him with obedience, regardless of the cost. So the first step in understanding and accepting His call is just that—declaring that you will accept it.

## Fully Appreciate the Cost and Be Willing to Pay It

It might seem as if you should fully appreciate the cost of God's calling before accepting it. But experience has shown me that no matter how long I take to assess the cost of obedience, I don't fully appreciate it until I make my unwavering declaration to follow.

So what will compel us to not only declare our commitment to Christ, but also to actually pay the cost of following Him? God has shown me that often my delay in following Jesus boils down to the question Jesus asked Peter three times in John 21: "Do you love me?"

Could it really be that simple? Is accepting the cost really just about settling in our hearts if we love Him? God showed me the answer to this through my own personal life. If my husband or sons were ill, would I not spare any expense to help them recover? Would I not reprioritize my schedule to get them to the hospital? Would I not cut expenses wherever I could to be able to pay for their care? Would I spend one second analyzing whether I would pay the cost? In my answers to those questions, I answer the question of whether or not I love them. I would do what I needed to do, no matter the cost, because I love them.

Few people question how much of themselves, their time, and their resources they will give their children or grandchildren. Few parents would hesitate to give a kidney to their dying child. Yet when it comes to giving God what He longs for, we often find ourselves setting a ceiling on our affections, which effectually tells Him that we don't really love Him—our Father and King. We must be willing to pay the cost in order to follow God's call.

## Acknowledge God's Power

After we declare our commitment to God and decide that we are willing to pay the cost no matter what, we need to realize that the only way we can give God what He desires is through leaning on Him and trusting in His power. If we try to do it on our own, we will surely fail. It is through His strength that we can actually pay the cost of our calling.

I knew a woman who wrestled with God when He first called her to serve in the ministry. She accepted the call. She understood clearly how much her calling would cost her, and she took the leap of faith of accepting it. She felt very surrendered until she got to stage three. Part of the cost was leaving corporate America to serve God full-time in ministry. She asked God to part the Red Sea by providing for her financially before she cut the umbilical cord from her corporate job. As I watched her wrestle with her decision, I knew from observing God's patterns that He was not going to provide for her until she stopped trying to solve challenges in her own power. She was using her own human logic to solve the problem and determined she did not know anyone who could support her. She tried to make ends meet through her own savings and ran short. Meanwhile, God had connections throughout the city but she never once asked God to lead her to His connections. As a result, she stayed in corporate America and missed God's divine appointment.

In her human capability, she was not able to have the level of faith that would trust God with new ways to provide for her future finances. It is when we humble ourselves before

God and acknowledge His power over all things that He will then carry us to a level beyond our wildest imagination. He knows all things, and He knows that even in demonstrating faith, we are unable to love Him the way we thought we could. It is at this place that He then shows us that He will receive what we are able to give and begin to do great things through us.

Let's look at an example of this in the life of a member of our royal family tree. When Jesus asked Peter if he loved Him, He asked the question three times. The first time, Jesus said, "Simon son of John, do you truly love me more than these?" (John 21:15). The word Jesus used for "love" in this question was the Greek word *agapao*, which is a decision to love—the same kind of love that led Jesus to finish His work on the cross. There are times when we do not feel like loving, but we do so as an act of our choice and will. That is *agapao* love. Peter's answer to this question was, "Yes, Lord, . . . you know that I love you" (John 21:15). But the Greek word for love that Peter used was *phileo*, which is a friendship type of love, clearly not one as intense as what Jesus was asking for.

In John 21:16, Jesus asked Peter a second time, "Simon son of John, do you truly love me?" Again, He used the word *agapao*. And Peter again answered with *phileo*. Then an incredible thing happened. Jesus asked Peter the question a third time, but this time He used the word *phileo* instead of *agapao*. He confirmed Peter's admission that he could not, in his own power, do what was asked of him. So God went to where Peter was. It is the same with us. When we humble ourselves before Him and acknowledge our human weaknesses, He meets us where we are and then He grows us into what He is asking of us.

## When God Says Move . . . MOVE

After we understand and accept God's calling for us and acknowledge that it can only be done through His power, it's time to act. When God calls us, He is ready to take over a situation. And this is the point where we find out exactly what the cost is. There will be no more counting the cost—there just *is* the cost.

Mark 1:19–20 tells us, "When he had gone a little farther, he saw James son of Zebedee and his brother John in a boat, preparing their nets. Without delay he called them, and they left their father Zebedee in the boat with the hired men and followed him." What did James and John leave behind? They left behind their jobs, their boat, . . . and their father. Now that's a big cost. We don't know what Zebedee thought about all of this, but can you imagine what he was thinking as his two sons left him standing in the boat? And there were probably times when James and John missed their dad and missed fishing. In fact, where did Jesus find them, not long after He had appeared to them in the upper room after His resurrection? In a boat—trying to catch some fish.

But the point is that when God is ready to move, He expects us to follow even if it means leaving jobs, the ones we love, and our assets. Hebrews 10:34–39 says:

> You sympathized with those in prison and joyfully accepted the confiscation of your property, because you knew that you yourselves had better and lasting possessions. So do not throw away your confidence; it will be richly rewarded. You need to persevere so that when you have done the will of God, you will receive what he has promised. For in just a very little while, "He who is coming will come and will not delay. But my righteous one will live by faith. And if he shrinks back, I will not be pleased with him." But we are not of those who shrink back and are destroyed, but of those who believe and are saved.

Did you notice the words "joyfully accepted the confiscation of your property"? Would you be able to *joyfully* accept the loss of everything you own if that is what following God cost you? But we must also look at the next words: "because you knew that you yourselves had better and lasting possessions." As daughters of the King, we have the priceless possessions of salvation, eternal life, and future reward. God wants us to have blessings that no event or human can steal from us.

Also observe how God states that those who are righteous will live by faith—not by human logic. It goes against human logic to give up everything for a "cause." But God expects us to follow Him regardless of the cost. He even says, "And if he shrinks back, I will not be pleased with him."

In order to follow God, we must be willing to give up anything and everything. If He is silent in your life, is it because you are unwilling to give something up? What won't you let go of that has consumed you and kept you from answering God's call?

## Stay on Course during the Storms

God's silences do not just come at the beginning of a call or as we consider the cost of following. They also come as we are in the trenches, faithfully doing the work He has called us to do. It would seem that when, as God's daughters, we are doing exactly what He has called us to, we should not feel alone in the storms we will inevitably face. Yet often, even when we are in the center of His will, God will be silent.

Jesus' disciples experienced this. Consider the following story:

> That day when evening came, he said to his disciples, "Let us go over to the other side." Leaving the crowd behind, they took him along, just as he was, in the boat. There were also other boats with him. A furious squall came up, and the waves broke over the boat, so that it was nearly

swamped. Jesus was in the stern, sleeping on a cushion. The disciples woke him and said to him, "Teacher, don't you care if we drown?" He got up, rebuked the wind and said to the waves, "Quiet! Be still!" Then the wind died down and it was completely calm. (Mark 4:35–39)

Observe that it was while the disciples were on a journey with Jesus that the storm arose. It was Jesus' idea to go to the other side of the lake. He told them to go, He fell asleep, and the storm came up. Do you ever feel like God has gone to sleep when you're dealing with a storm along the path *He* sent you down? You find yourself saying, "Wait a minute! This was Your idea! So where are You in the middle of this storm?"

We tend to believe that when we are where God wants us to be, we will feel secure. Although the safest place to be is in the middle of God's will, it won't always *feel* safe. Our human tendency is to panic when storms appear. The disciples panicked—they thought they were going to drown—even with Jesus Himself in their boat. They even accused Jesus of not caring about them. But notice that before responding to their accusation, Jesus calmed the storm. He met their immediate, physical need, and *then* He dealt with their lack of faith. "Why are you so afraid? Do you still have no faith?" (Mark 4:40).

*Still.* Even if we didn't know that the disciples had a history of not trusting Jesus, that one word—*still*—tells us that this was not the first time, and that it most likely wouldn't be the last. They had seen Him heal many people and cast out demons, yet they still didn't trust Him. We don't have the luxury of seeing Jesus' miracles performed while He was on earth, like the disciples did. But whether or not we personally have experienced a miracle in our lives, we all know what Jesus did for us on the cross.

We know that Jesus died a horrible death for us. We also know that He could have called legions of angels to deliver Him. But He stayed on the cross to ensure the full payment of our sins so that God could offer us the gift of eternal life. God sent us His Son to protect the dream He had for us to reign with Him forever as His sons and daughters. What else do we think we need God to do before we will trust Him?

The next time we see those black clouds rolling across the sky, instead of accusing God, let's choose to trust Him and not panic. In the midst of the storm, we can rest assured that God is not in a panic. He knew about the storm even before it showed up on our radar screen. In due time, we will hear Him say, "Quiet! Be still!" and the storm will pass. Meanwhile, what God wants us to do is stay on course. Don't throw out your calling every time you encounter a challenge.

I wish I could tell you that God speaks clearly and consistently, but there are many days when I can't hear Him. Yet that doesn't mean I should just give it up. I believe that often God uses those times of silence to see if I will trust Him more. When I know that I am on the path God has called me to, yet He is silent, I simply proceed through any open door I can find. I don't stop because He isn't speaking. Even when no doors seem to be open, I can't give up on His dream.

As I look back over the years at Inspire Women, I remember many times I just wanted to crawl into bed and never wake up because of God's silence during the storms. Yet all the while, I felt a strong conviction that I was doing exactly what God wanted. I knew that God was watching over me and that He wanted to know if He could trust me to keep going even when He was silent.

I have learned that the more we walk with God, the more faith He expects from us. As God conforms us to Jesus' image, He will walk us into times when He is intentionally silent and He will watch to see if we stay on course and keep doing the last thing we heard Him tell us to do.

# How God Used the Storms
## in My Life to Display His Power

Some of the biggest storms in my life have been just that—rainstorms. After we moved into our house, we discovered that the people of our neighborhood had been fighting with the city for years to fix a drainage problem that occasionally caused the houses to flood during storms. When I heard that a big storm was coming our way while I was preparing to leave town to speak to 2,000 women at a conference in another city, my first thought was that God would not allow my house to flood under those circumstances. I couldn't imagine having to leave my family in a flooded home while I went off to a conference.

However, as I listened to the rain, I realized that the harder the rain hit the roof, the faster my heart pounded. The softer the rain fell, the more I relaxed. It hit me that I had attached my emotional peace of mind to my environment. I was going up and down on an emotional roller coaster based on what was happening around me. It is one thing to have preferences for the conditions of your environment, but it is sin when we rely on our environment as the dictating factor to our sense of security. I realized that I needed to put my trust in God instead of my environment.

As soon as God redirected my trust to Him alone, the most amazing thing happened. He allowed our house to flood. I could not believe that God was sending me to speak at an out-of-town conference when our house was underwater. Why had He not answered my prayer to keep our house from flooding? Why had He slept while my boat was going under?

I later realized that my convenience was not God's priority. His priority was to send me as His voice to share His hope with those who were seeking answers for their lives. Those women were hurting, and God couldn't send a speaker to them who was untouched by life.

When I told the audience that my house was under water, many were encouraged by my misery. It surprises me sometimes how we can be more of an encouragement in our misery than in our success. It is our power—through Christ—in the midst of our weakness that gets the world's attention. We see this in Paul's life.

> To keep me from becoming conceited because of these surpassingly great revelations, there was given me a thorn in my flesh, a messenger of Satan, to torment me. Three times I pleaded with the Lord to take it away from me. But he said to me, "My grace is sufficient for you, for my power is made perfect in weakness." (2 Corinthians 12:7–9)

God really does use the storms to display His power—the literal storms and the symbolic ones. Like Paul's thorn in the flesh, my storms seemed never-ending as well. At times we thought God would never deliver us from them.

The first time, it took nine months to get everything repaired. When it happened the second time, I told the Lord I didn't have the energy to deal with it. But I did deal with it. By the third time, I was a pro. And then the city finally repaired the road to solve the drainage problem. As I watched the workers install the big drainage pipes, I thought about how God comes through for us even when we think He's not paying attention.

When the work was finished, the neighborhood threw a party in celebration, and no one was more excited than the Carman family. God had delivered us from the storm, and we were not afraid to give Him the praise in front of our neighbors. Then a week later, another rain came . . . and out of all the houses in the neighborhood, only ours flooded. When we wondered what had happened, some of the neighbors said, "God sent the rain. Why don't you talk to your God about why this happened?" I said to the Lord, as I had each time before,

"Why is it that after you part the Red Sea, I turn the corner and there is another Red Sea?" He responded, "To see if you will panic this time. If you've gone through one Red Sea, your faith should be stronger for the next one."

God watches for our responses to our circumstances—and so do our neighbors, coworkers, and people involved in our ministries. It was not a coincidence that each of those floods occurred the week before I was to give the keynote address at the Inspire Women Conference. God used my suffering to inspire the women at each of those conferences. His silences and delays in response to our pleas to stop the flooding served a purpose. He wanted to teach me—and the conference attendees—that we need to manage our environment instead of letting it manage us. He showed His power through the storms.

By the way, the city came in with a second phase of work to repair the drainage again. And it worked. The city brought in huge pipes the same year Inspire Women was raising an endowed scholarship fund. I watched the work crew dig deep trenches and put the pipes in place the month before the campaign's projected completion date. During a time when I had no idea how God would finish the campaign, the timing of the drainage pipes became God's tangible evidence to me that He always finishes what He begins. At the end of the day, the moral of the story is this: This storm, too, shall pass. All storms do.

# Section 2

# *Transforming Rejection*

## TO FULFILL GOD'S PURPOSE

WHEN THE BIBLE SPEAKS of rejection, it is almost always in the context of one of the following two circumstances: either the people were rejecting God, or He was vowing not to reject them in return. For instance, in Leviticus 26:43–45, God says:

> They will pay for their sins because they rejected my laws and abhorred my decrees. Yet in spite of this, when they are in the land of their enemies, I will not reject them or abhor them so as to destroy them completely, breaking my covenant with them. I am the Lord their God. But for their sake I will remember the covenant with their ancestors whom I brought out of Egypt in the sight of the nations to be their God. I am the Lord.

If someone has rejected you for missing the mark, realize that the Israelites missed the mark in God's books over and over again. Know that even though the world may give up on you, God will continue to give you another chance, just as He did for His people long ago.

Rejection of God wasn't just limited to the Old

Testament Israelites. In the New Testament, we read Jesus' words to His disciples, "The Son of Man must suffer many things and be rejected by the elders, chief priests and teachers of the law, and he must be killed and on the third day be raised to life" (Luke 9:22). We know that Jesus' words came true. He was rejected by man like no other man has been. If you feel like you have sacrificially laid down your life for someone only to have them reject you and hurt you, know that you serve a God who experienced a worse rejection, to the point of being nailed to a cross.

Throughout Scripture, we see that God repeatedly loves us, affirms us, and claims us for Himself despite the fact that we reject Him on a consistent basis. However, instead of taking strength from that belief, we often fall prey to the devil's schemes to distort our self-image and make us crumble under the weight of our own rejection. Satan loves to watch us crush each other through misunderstandings, unjust criticism, and emotional abuse. He watches in glee as we become human missiles that put each other out of commission for use in God's kingdom by sending messages of rejection.

It is clear that this should not be the code of conduct for God's royal family. We come from a line of faith heroes who did not allow rejection to change their appointed missions. When you rise above rejection, you are acting as a true daughter of the King of Kings.

These next four chapters will lead you through a process of pinpointing the different areas of your life where you might face rejection: in your family, in your community, and in your ministry or workplace. We will wrap up the section by specifically looking at how to overcome defeat when your sense of calling is rejected.

Has God given you a dream that you are not chasing because of rejection in your past? Know that God has allowed every incident of your life to shape you into the perfect vessel that He needs for the mission He has called you to. He will not send you out to do something He knows you can't accomplish. God can take even the heartache caused by rejection and transform it into a passionate purpose for Him.

As guardians of dreams for a family, business, church, ministry, community, or nation, we must allow God to give us *His* vision for our lives and stick to them no matter what sort of rejection we face. This is the way of the royal family.

# Chapter 5

## When Your

### FAMILY REJECTS YOU

"You intended to harm me, but
God intended it for good."

Genesis 50:20

*T*he wounds inflicted on us during childhood
cut deep. When those wounds are the result
of family members and loved ones who abused their
influence over us during our formative years, they can
seem almost debilitating. Whether you were physically abandoned, physically or emotionally abused, or
simply neglected, rejection by family members can
leave lifelong scars.

Rejection isn't always blatant, however. Often-
times, it is very subtle. As a child, were you rarely or
never affirmed? Were you never encouraged to
dream? Were you self-conscious about using your talents or abilities for fear of being accused of being ambitious? Did your parents favor one of your siblings
over you? These are subtle forms of rejection that
often go unnoticed by others and are often ignored,
but they can be very detrimental to our spiritual and
emotional health.

When family members reject us, it is as if someone burned negative tracks in our memory bank that have the power to distort our view of ourselves for the rest of our lives. Some numb the pain through drugs. Others escape into a fantasy world of their own making. Still others cry silently on the inside while acting like a carefree spirit on the outside. And some simply check out of life and no longer care to make a difference.

With these coping mechanisms, we may experience some relief, but we start to feel empty because we are disconnected from our divine mission. We were never meant to sit on the bench! We were meant to get up, get out onto the court, and make a difference! But before we can step into God's purpose for our lives, He has to transform our poor self-image into a true self-image and erase those negative tapes from childhood.

## God Looks at the Heart

I grew up in an environment of scarcity. Although my parents tried to give me all that I needed, the fact that there was so little to spare made me feel that any need I had was an intrusion. On the day I turned ten, nobody said anything to me about it being my birthday. When we're in the twilight of life, we might breathe a sigh of relief that nobody acknowledged that we are another year older. However, it was devastating to a ten-year-old girl. Late in the day, my mother noticed that I was unhappy, and I told her it was because I hadn't received a birthday gift. Since she didn't have money to shop for me, she borrowed some from a neighbor and went out and bought me a brightly painted aluminum chicken that would cluck, spin in circles, and even lay eggs. I thought it was wonderful ... until my father came home and found out what had happened. Money was tight, and he was irritated by what had happened. As a result, I felt guilty and began to think of myself as a burden to the family.

At one point, my mother even told me that her pregnancy with me was unwanted and unwelcome because of what my needs meant to the family's finances. Those words scarred the first chapters of my life. I felt like a bad beginning that the world had to put up with.

Since I was an unwelcome and unwanted part of my family, it stands to reason that I had a very low self-image. If my own family didn't want me, who would? However, God taught me from His Word that the only image I needed to concern myself with is God's image of me. Genesis 1:27 says, "So God created man in his own image, in the image of God he created him; male and female he created them." Therefore, since God made us to reflect His image, we should get our self-image from God and not from anyone else. In fact, anyone else who tries to give us an image that falls short of our royal heritage offends God and usurps His authority. All human opinion falls by the wayside when God has spoken.

This truth can be seen in the story of Samuel anointing one of Jesse's sons as the king who would replace Saul, the first King of Israel. In this story in 1 Samuel 16, God shows us how God makes up His own mind about people and totally ignores the opinions of their families.

God had told Samuel that He had chosen one of Jesse's sons to be the next king, but He initially didn't tell him which one. When the oldest son stood in front of Samuel, his appearance alone made Samuel think he was the chosen one (1 Samuel 16:6). But God warned Samuel against such thinking. He knew that fallen humanity tends to accept or reject people based on outward appearances. So God said to Samuel, "Do not consider his appearance or his height, for I have rejected him. The Lord does not look at the things man looks at. Man looks at the outward appearance, but the Lord looks at the heart" (1 Samuel 16:7). With this instruction, Samuel sought God's confirmation as he evaluated the rest of Jesse's sons. Samuel's message to each of the other six sons was some version of this: "The Lord has not chosen this one either" (1 Samuel 16:8). We can almost feel Samuel's frustration as, after each of Jesse's sons standing before him was rejected, he said to Jesse, "The Lord has not chosen these. . . . Are these all the sons you have?" (1 Samuel 16:10–11).

Jesse's answer to this question revealed his opinion of his youngest son, David: "There is still the youngest, . . . but he is tending the sheep." Jesse showed his heart and his personal evaluation of his sons by not even considering that the youngest, the shepherd who spent his days alone tending his father's flock, could be Israel's next king. But God saw something different in David. When this young man appeared in front of Samuel, God said, "Rise and anoint him; he is the one" (1 Samuel 16:12). How incredible that the one rejected by man was the one God had chosen!

Samuel didn't have the final say in who would be king, and neither did Jesse. "He is the one" were *God's* words. There is incredible peace in knowing that God has the final word. It matters little what parents or siblings or little-known acquaintances think of you. It only matters what God thinks of you. He sees your heart, just as He saw David's. The apostle Paul wrote: "After removing Saul, he made David their king. He testified concerning him: 'I have found David son of Jesse a man after my own heart; he will do everything I want him to do'" (Acts 13:22).

When God has an assignment that is close to His heart, He will pick the one He can trust. If God has chosen you, shut your ears to the opinions around you. No matter how difficult the assignment, remind yourself, "I am the one. I am the one God picked and God never makes a mistake."

There is another thing to learn from the 1 Samuel 16 passage. You don't have to go looking for God's will. God knows where you live. Thousands of years ago, He sent Samuel to invite David to step into a divine appointment. David was out in the pastures taking care of the sheep, and he was maybe even already writing beautiful poetry like we find in the Psalms. God wouldn't have chosen David unless He was already purifying him. Scripture tells us that God is in search of a holy vessel with a heart that is willing to serve Him. Second Timothy 2:20–21 reads: "In a large house there are articles not only of gold and silver, but also of wood and clay; some are for noble purposes and some for ignoble. If a man cleanses himself from the latter, he will be an instrument for noble purposes, made holy, useful to the Master and prepared to do any good work." When we focus on getting the vessel ready, God then comes with the assignment.

Are you an instrument for noble purposes? If so, then God knows where you live. He is perfectly able to intersect your path to point you where He wants to take you. The question is, when God knocks on your door, will you recognize that heaven has invaded earth?

## Don't Forget Who the True Enemy Is

Whenever you have been appointed to do a great work for God, you will be challenged by Satan. In fact, the more impact you were designed to have, the stronger the attack you can expect to come your way.

Perhaps you have suffered from domestic abuse from the hands of those you trusted as your authority figures. Realize that incidents from your past will also be your current vulnerabilities. Therefore, when you find yourself responding emotionally to an incident, ask yourself if your reaction is proportional to what has happened. Be alert to the fact that you might have walked into a trap set up by the devil to bring back the pain of your past to disable you from making good decisions in the present.

When you have distrust issues with authority figures from your past, what better way can Satan knock you off course than to plant doubt in your mind about the people who are currently in authority over you. He will do whatever he can to make you not trust godly leaders who are trying to help and guide you. He will manipulate you into living with the belief that you have to protect your own future in order to survive. Instead, God wants us to be strong and stand up against Satan: "Finally, be strong in the Lord and in his mighty power. Put on the full armor of God so that you can take your stand against the devil's schemes. For our struggle is not against flesh and blood, but against the rulers, against the authorities, against the powers of this dark world and against the spiritual forces of evil in the heavenly realms" (Ephesians 6:10–12). Know who you are in Christ, and don't let Satan bring you down.

Because of rejection in your past, your whole psyche may be geared toward being safe. If you allow this to happen, at the end of your life, you may be safe, but you will have missed your divine purpose and those God sent your way to grow you in maturity. Samuel was a godly leader who spoke truth into David's life. Paul spoke truth into Timothy's life. Find a leader you can trust, and then submit to their instruction and trust their guidance. Don't let Satan take away the Samuels and Pauls in your own life.

## Forgive, and You Will Be Forgiven

Another important aspect of transforming rejection is forgiveness. This is the way of the royal family, and we see it in the story of Joseph. Through Joseph's life, we see that rejection by your family doesn't always come from your parents—sibling rivalry can also cause harsh rejection. In Joseph's case, *he* was the favored child: "Now Israel loved Joseph more than any of his other sons" (Genesis 37:3). Therefore, it is quite understandable that his brothers wouldn't be very happy with him. In addition, Joseph had two dreams that predicted that one day his brothers and parents would bow down to him and that he would reign over them (Genesis 37:5–9). When Joseph told his brothers about these dreams, they disliked him even more.

Have you ever shared your dreams with your siblings, thinking they would rejoice with you, but instead they accused you of thinking you were better than them and you discovered they couldn't wait for you to fail? That's what happened to Joseph. Joseph's brothers rejected him in the worst way. The story continues as follows:

> So Joseph went after his brothers and found them near Dothan. But they saw him in the distance, and before he reached them, they plotted to kill him. "Here comes that dreamer!" they said to each other. "Come now, let's kill him and throw him into one of these cisterns and say that a ferocious animal devoured him. Then we'll see what comes of his dreams." . . . Judah said to his brothers, "What will we gain if we kill our brother and cover up his blood? Come, let's sell him to the Ishmaelites and not lay our hands on him; after all, he is our brother, our own flesh and blood." His brothers agreed. (Genesis 37:17–20, 26–27)

In order to cover up what they did, Joseph's brothers soaked his robe in goat's blood and gave it to their father, telling him that a ferocious animal had killed Joseph. Genesis 37:34–35 records, "Then Jacob tore his clothes, put on sackcloth and mourned for his son many days. All his sons and daughters came to comfort him, but he refused to be comforted." Have you ever been disgusted by how your siblings wanted the credit for comforting your parents when actually they were the ones who caused your parents' deepest distress? Do you find your siblings' hypocrisy eating you up on the inside?

Maybe you have been in a situation where family members manipulated events to throw you out of the family. But for Joseph, that wasn't the end of the story, and that doesn't have to be the end of your story, either.

Joseph was taken to Egypt, and throughout a series of circumstances over many years, God used his ability to interpret dreams to elevate him to second-in-command over all of Egypt. Through Joseph's interpretation of one of Pharaoh's dreams, the nation of Egypt was warned about a coming famine, and they were able to store up enough food to get them through. However, back in the land of Canaan, where Joseph's family lived, they had no way of knowing about the famine and so they weren't prepared. When they heard that there was grain to be found in Egypt, they went there, and who did they meet? Joseph—the brother they had sold into slavery.

If you were Joseph, how would you have responded to your brothers' plea for food? Would you have sent them away to starve? Would you have grudgingly given them some and sent them packing? Or would you have done what Joseph did—forgive them? Take a look at what happened.

> When Joseph's brothers saw that their father was dead, they said, "What if Joseph holds a grudge against us and pays us back for all the wrongs we did to him?" So they sent word to Joseph, saying, "Your father left these instructions before he died: 'This is what you are to say to Joseph: I ask you to forgive your brothers the sins and the wrongs they committed in treating you so badly.' Now please forgive the sins of the servants of the God of your father." When their message came to him, Joseph wept. His brothers then came and threw themselves down before him. "We are your slaves," they said. But Joseph said to them, "Don't be afraid. Am I in the place of God? You intended to harm me, but God intended it for good to accomplish what is now being done, the saving of many lives. So then, don't be afraid. I will provide for you and your children." And he reassured them and spoke kindly to them. (Genesis 50:15–21)

When your parent is no longer alive and there is no parent to compete for or to impress, how will you choose to respond to the wrong your siblings committed against you? Joseph could have made his brothers his slaves—he could have punished them for what they did to him all those years ago. Instead, he chose to forgive them, provide for their families, and be kind to them. Are you ready to forgive and be kind to those family members who have rejected you? They may never ask for your forgiveness. They may not acknowledge that they did anything wrong. What then is your motive to forgive? We forgive because forgiveness is the royal way—it is the way a daughter of the King responds because forgiveness flows in our veins. Psalm 103:12 tells us, "As far as the east is from the west, so far has he removed our transgressions from us." We serve a heavenly Father who offers us total forgiveness. Out of the overflow of His love for us, we can forgive others.

Ultimately, God wants us to know that no matter what family dynamics we have experienced, He is our heavenly Father who created us in His image. When we act like our heavenly Father, we express our identity as His daughter. He wants us to operate out of the image He gave us, not one distorted by rejection. The only voice He wants us to listen for is His voice. And He wants us to hear His affirmation that we are His beloved, in whom He is well pleased.

## How God Transformed My Past

At the heart of the ministry of Inspire Women is the mission to inspire women from all ethnic backgrounds, denominations, and economic levels to step into God's purpose. As proof of the seriousness with which we believe in the potential of God's daughters, Inspire Women funds scholarships to train those called to missions and ministry.

The astounding facts of the way God established Inspire Women provided evidence of God's power to transform any background. He picked a founder with deep wounds of rejection by parents who didn't want her to be born, a mother who took her own life, and a culture that esteemed male children more than female ones. There are incidents in our lives that we can logically think and talk through and get past, but when the wounds are emotional and deep, certain incidents continue to trigger our pain. Yet, God intentionally chose one with a wounded background to show His daughters that He can shape anyone for His passionate purposes.

At the crossroads of my life, I had to decide if I would allow the messages of rejection from my background to determine my self-image and limit how I served God, or if I would allow God to have the final word. It was after studying the story of Samuel anointing David that I learned that if someone godly invites you to do something, take it seriously. And this belief led to me making a decision that changed the course of my life.

God did not want me to live with the self-image I developed in my childhood, so He put a godly leader in my life to transform the image developed from memories of rejection into His purpose for me. As I have mentioned before, God brought me to Houston and placed me under a godly leader— Beth Moore. One day Beth called and asked me if I could teach her Sunday school class of nearly three hundred women. I could not imagine why she had called me. I had never expressed a desire to teach. I didn't believe I had the gift of teaching, and I was happy to simply sit under her teaching every week. So why in the world did she call me?

God was using Beth to change my image of myself. I had learned from His Word that when someone filled with God's Spirit invites you to do something, you should take it seriously. By faith in God's Word as the direction for my life, I submitted to the fact that God leads us through godly leaders. So I taught the class. I was sure it would be the only time I would teach, thinking that God was simply testing me to see if I would do it. My own self-image was disconnected from God's view of me. I was surprised when I was invited to teach at a women's retreat. Beth was in the audience. After I spoke, she came up to me and said, "I don't know how to tell you this, but I believe God has called you to be a speaker."

I trusted Beth's word for my life and decided that if God called me to teach His Word, then I ought to get some preparation and education. So I enrolled at Dallas Theological Seminary. When I graduated, I was surprised to discover I had graduated top of my class. God, in His mercy, was giving me ammunition to combat the old tapes from my background. He is perfectly able to put His seal of blessing on you, as well, to show the world He is proud of His daughter whom He trusts with His mission.

# Chapter 6

## *When Your*

### COMMUNITY
### REJECTS YOU

"For you are all one in Christ
Jesus."

Galatians 3:28

*P*eople are most comfortable with others who look like them, act like them, and think like them. That's all well and good if you are surrounded by people who are just like you, but what if you're not? What about those times and places where you're different from the others? Do you ever feel like your community or culture is constantly playing a game of "one of these things is not like the others," and the "one" they always pick out is you?

Maybe you look different than everyone else because of your race or a disability. Perhaps you act differently because you grew up in a different culture than they did. Or it could be that you think differently than they do because of the unique experiences of your life. But no matter the cause, being rejected by your community—whether it's a neighborhood, a town, a workplace, or even a church—makes you feel like you don't fit in this world.

# Rejected Because of
# Gender or Race

Growing up in Hong Kong, I was a second-class citizen in two ways. First, I was a girl, and girls are seen as inferior to boys in traditional Chinese culture. Second, I was a citizen of a British colony—not Great Britain itself. Unlike those born in the British Isles, the citizens of Hong Kong were given inferior passports with restricted travel privileges.

This concept of inferior citizenship followed me through different arenas of my life. As a result, it amazed me that God picked *me*—with my fragile heart and often negative self-image—to lead the charge in a ministry area with a high potential for rejection. I have seen how many people who were brought up in an affirming environment are able to let rejection roll off their backs, so it only seemed logical to me that someone like that should lead this ministry instead of me.

God had to do much repair work in my heart before He could trust me with a mission to affirm the potential of women to change the world. After all, how could I support and encourage anyone when I felt like a misfit? I didn't grow up in a culture that affirmed the potential of women. I was not raised to believe I could make much of a difference in the world. The deep imprint of scripts that others had handed me had to be rewritten with the pen of God's mighty Word. God had to create in me a correct concept about how He feels about His daughters.

First, I had to learn that our race does not make us either inferior or superior. The apostle Paul tells us in Galatians 3:28, "There is neither Jew nor Greek, slave nor free, male nor female, for you are all one in Christ Jesus." We are *all* one. Not just some of us, *all* of us. Even though earthly kingdoms might decide that one race or group of people is more important than another, that is not true in God's kingdom.

Next, God had to teach me that being a daughter is not a

lower calling than being a son. Genesis 1:27 reads, "So God created man in his own image, in the image of God he created him; male and female he created them." In this verse, God tells us that all humankind was created to represent God on this earth. Although we may have different roles, we must rise above the artificial limitations we impose on each other. The belief that one gender or one race has greater potential than all others to represent God's image on earth is not substantiated in Scripture. When we create artificial ceilings for each other, we block God's image from being fully expressed in the world.

God has equally blessed men and women. In Genesis 5:1–2, we read that "when God created man, he made him in the likeness of God. He created them male and female and blessed them. And when they were created, he called them 'man.'" These verses show us that God defines the word "man" to include both male and female. He tells us that He blessed *them*, not just *him*. It is very eye opening to read that from the very beginning of creation, God valued both male and female and saw that they, as a united force, would represent God as "man" on earth.

## "Both Men and Women"

Even though God created both men and women in His own image, it is not uncommon for women to feel rejected by the church—especially women who feel called to minister to others. If or where a line should be drawn between what men can do and what women can do in the church is not the issue here. The issue is that God has called both men and women to serve Him and to spread His gospel among the nations. When Jesus gave the Great Commission to His disciples, He was speaking to a group of men at that moment, but His words were written down in Scripture for all of us, not just males.

God never meant for women to be left out of ministry. When it comes to how we should serve, God taught me to ask the question, "Who will be the first to die for Christ?" If this question is answered, all other roles will fall into place. When your heart attitude is one of service instead of rights or titles, you will find yourself praising and serving God wherever you find yourself, wherever there is a need, and wherever God sends you to save the perishing.

Time is too precious and the need too urgent for arguments among those who are saved while billions are dying without hearing the gospel. And rest assured that if you are trying to spread God's Word—whether male or female—there will be those who will try to silence you. Luke 19:37–40 speaks to this:

> When he came near the place where the road goes down the Mount of Olives, the whole crowd of disciples began joyfully to praise God in loud voices for all the miracles they had seen: "Blessed is the king who comes in the name of the Lord!" "Peace in heaven and glory in the highest!" Some of the Pharisees in the crowd said to Jesus, "Teacher, rebuke your disciples!" "I tell you," he replied, "if they keep quiet, the stones will cry out."

Like the Pharisees in Jesus' day, there will always be those who reject you and demand your silence. But we must not keep silent in proclaiming the Good News, because the time may well be short. Only God knows when time on planet Earth will be over. He alone knows when the last day will come for those who have not heard the gospel. He knows when He will unleash the potential of all believers to shout His message to the world before the curtain falls on the earth and the opportunity to accept the gift of Jesus has passed.

In Acts 2:17–18 we read, "In the last days, God says, I will pour out my Spirit on all people. Your sons and daughters will prophesy, your young men will see visions, your old men will dream dreams. Even on my servants, both men and women, I will pour out my Spirit in those days, and they will prophesy." Peter spoke those words on the day of Pentecost, when the believers received the gift of the Holy Spirit. At that time, women lived in a culture where biblical training was not available to them. So their potential was limited by what their culture allowed for their education. However, today, tradition has changed and our culture has lifted its limitations on educational opportunities based on gender and race. Communities of all types are more open to hear from "sons and daughters," "young and old," and they welcome "servants" who are filled with God's Spirit and are ready to pour out His hope to the world.

## The Real Battle

It is Christ who has made us acceptable to God. He is the one who pleases God. When we accept the blood of Jesus for the forgiveness of our sins, Christ places a covering over us with His sacrifice. When God looks at us, He no longer sees our imperfections but He sees Christ. In our human logic, we find ourselves arguing for the equality or superiority of gender or race. But in God's eyes, we are fighting the wrong battle. The ultimate question we must answer is how each of us compares to God's holiness, because this is the only decisive factor that will matter for our eternal destination.

It matters little how we compare to each other in characteristics such as gender or race. When it comes to anything of eternal significance, God evaluates us on the basis of holiness. In this regard, Romans 3:22–24 tells us, "There is no difference, for all have sinned and fall short of the glory of God, and are justified freely by his grace through the redemption that came by Christ Jesus."

Based on our holiness, we have all failed, whether male or

female, Jew or Greek, slave or free. We are all in the same boat of not quite making it according to God's standards. We are all saved by faith and offered the same gift of the blood of Jesus Christ as the full payment for the penalty of our sins. So when someone has the attitude that they are superior and they reject you based on gender, race, or something else they perceive as making you inferior, rest in the fact that God sees all as equal under the covering of the blood of His Son. We are all equal at the foot of the cross. Find strength in knowing that it is by the power of Jesus' blood that we will represent God's image on this earth. The criterion God uses to assess how well we can represent His image is our dependence on the holiness and power of His Son. All other criteria are man-made and misguided.

Think of it this way. You are reaching for a cookie jar on the top shelf and I tell you that you can't reach it because you're dressed in red. Perhaps I could even be persuasive enough to make you believe that your red clothes will actually affect your ability to reach the cookie jar. But the reality is that the color of your clothing has nothing to do with your ability to reach it. The premise is a misguided criterion. Your ability to reach the cookie jar is based on having the right ladder to reach the height you need to reach. Christ Jesus is our ladder to God. We belong to Him and it is only through Him that we will be part of a united community that represents God's purpose on earth.

## The Ultimate Unfairness

Have you ever felt you were rejected in favor of someone else who wasn't as "worthy" or qualified for a work project, ministry position, or other opportunity? Well, you're in good company, because Jesus suffered the ultimate unfairness. After His arrest, when He was placed before the crowds and they had the choice of freeing Him or a true criminal, He was not chosen. Matthew 27:20–23 tells the story.

But the chief priests and the elders persuaded the crowd to ask for Barabbas and to have Jesus executed. "Which of the two do you want me to release to you?" asked the governor. "Barabbas," they answered. "What shall I do, then, with Jesus who is called Christ?" Pilate asked. They all answered, "Crucify him!" "Why? What crime has he committed?" asked Pilate. But they shouted all the louder, "Crucify him!"

Barabbas was a criminal, and Jesus spent His entire life blessing others, yet it was Jesus who was rejected. How could it be that the crowds chose to release Barabbas instead of Christ? Because there was a hidden agenda. Those in leadership at the time were protecting their own interests. Their concern was not the people. It didn't seem to bother them that they were releasing a criminal who might cause more pain. All they cared about was protecting their benefits and their territory.

No matter how much Jesus blessed those around Him by healing the sick, the blind, the lame, and even raising the dead, He still faced a community who rejected Him because a few people wanted to protect themselves. The ones who experienced the blessings of Jesus were grateful to Him. It was the ones whose positions were threatened by Jesus' work who wanted to get rid of Him.

As a member of God's royal family, take some time to learn from your family's heritage. Observe what happened in Jesus' life that parallels your situation. When you are experiencing rejection, ask the questions, "Who is rejecting me, and why? What am I doing that threatens them? Do my activities take away from their importance?"

Those who opposed Jesus the most were the religious leaders of the day. It seems ironic that those who were supposedly closest to God were the ones who didn't recognize God Himself in their midst. However, as sinful humans, we all have the capability of doing the same thing. When we are more worried about protecting our own turf than we are about pleasing God, we run the risk of crushing those who are following Him and being obedient to His Word. So keep watch that you do not fall into the same trap as the Pharisees.

## The Royal Response

Have you ever received a verdict that changed the rest of your life? Perhaps your dream was to be a pediatrician, but every medical school rejected you. Or maybe you were wrongfully accused of abuse and your children were taken away from you and your community shunned you. Whether justified or not, the vote of a community can crush your world. But should it? How does the King want His children to respond to such situations?

If there was ever a person who was rejected by a community, it was Paul. He was rejected time and time again because of his message. On one of Paul's missionary journeys, he and Barnabas were in the city of Lystra. They were preaching the good news there, and Paul healed a man who had been crippled since birth. This amazed the people of Lystra, and Paul and Barnabas were able to tell them about their great God. But while they were there, a potentially disastrous situation arose. "Then some Jews came from Antioch and Iconium and won the crowd over. They stoned Paul and dragged him outside the city, thinking he was dead" (Acts 14:19). Did you notice that a few disgruntled people were able to win over an entire community against Paul to the point that they decided to kill him?

While you may never be the object of a murderous crowd, you may face situations when one or more people are able to effectively turn your entire community, church, or workplace against you. Under those circumstances, what would you do? Would you walk away and never go back? Perhaps that is what

God would lead you to do, but don't assume that is what He always wants. Let's look at what Paul did. After leaving Lystra, he and Barnabas went to the city of Derbe. "They preached the good news in [Derbe] and won a large number of disciples. Then they returned to Lystra, Iconium, and Antioch, strengthening the disciples and encouraging them to remain true to the faith" (Acts 14:21–22). In fulfillment of his mission, Paul returned to the very communities that rejected him so that he could strengthen and encourage the disciples there. He didn't allow Satan's attacks to throw him off course. This may be the same in your case. God might lead you to walk right back into a community that rejected you in order to accomplish His mission.

The devil wants us to believe that our circumstances control our reality. But this is not God's reality. What Satan tries to kill, God restores in ways that astound the world. God's story is one of displaying His resurrection power over what the devil tries to bury.

In the midst of the worst rejection in the history of the world, when God's one and only Son was wrongfully sentenced to death and nailed to a cross, God brought about the greatest victory on planet Earth. Jesus was not responsible for the choices of those who voted against Him, but He was responsible for how He responded to it. And His response was to keep going in His mission through whatever door was open. He kept going down to the last minute when He blessed His mother and committed her to the care of His beloved disciple John. In His final moments on earth, Jesus ministered to the needs of others and was the blessing God sent Him to be.

It is extremely freeing to know that God makes the final verdict in our lives. No one can throw us out of God's plans for us. We don't ever need the approval of a community to fulfill God's purpose. When God has allowed a rejection that has catastrophically affected our lives, remember the examples in our spiritual heritage. Jesus deserved to be King, but instead He was nailed to a cross. From the depths of His greatest rejection, Jesus rose above the darkness to save the world. This is the royal way. This can be your way if you live as a daughter of the King.

## How God Led Me
## through Rejection to Victory

As you already know, being a daughter in my native land of Hong Kong made me sorry I wasn't born a son. It was the sons—the men—who were esteemed as more important because they continued the family's name.

My mother had a son from her first marriage who left for the United States on a scholarship when I was three. I always felt like the little sister who was trying to pedal as fast as I could behind my brother. Over the years, God established my brother as a Senior Vice President for Fidelity Investments. He chose to take me on a different path and established me as the founder and president of Inspire Women. We were both created to be leaders. One was not better than the other. Both were God designed.

However, for a woman in leadership, success often creates opportunities for others to be critical. A man is never questioned about whether he is taking care of his children. But I hear through the grapevine about people making snide comments such as, "I wonder if her husband is happy. I'm sure her kids must be a mess." When I would not give up on God's projects, I was accused of being imbalanced while those who established new secular organizations were described as motivated. There were times when the only affirming voice I heard was that of my heavenly Father. In His grace, He surrounded me with a husband and two sons who continue to say to me, "Mom, eagles fly alone." I remember retorting, "I don't want to be an eagle, I want to be a chicken and cluck around with the rest of the crowd." One of my sons answered,

"The problem is, you don't get to choose. God is the one who has chosen." At the end of the day, leadership has a price. And God decides who will have the privilege to pay it.

It pains me to know that my mother didn't live to see how God transformed our family's dream for political freedom into a ministry that shares God's spiritual freedom. When her petition for immigration to the United States was denied, she allowed the rejection to take away her dreams. While there is still breath in me, I do not need to repeat my mother's choices. I can choose to rise above rejection and live in God's promises.

My prayer for you is that you will hold on to the dreams of your heavenly Father. Back in Genesis, when God said, "Let there be light," there was light (1:3). Whatever God speaks becomes a reality. When He whispers a dream for your life, He will carry you to finish what He began. Even when the world seems set against you, hold tightly to Him, stay on course, and believe that nothing can thwart His plans.

# Chapter 7

## *When Others*

### IN YOUR MINISTRY OR WORKPLACE REJECT YOU

"In everything he did he had great success, because the Lord was with him."

1 Samuel 18:14

In the workplace and ministry arenas, there are countless ways that we can be rejected. And we can be attacked from every direction—from our leaders, from our peers, and from those we lead.

Leaders might fear our success will threaten their position of authority, so they try to crush us. Peers may believe that our energy and new ideas will make them look inferior, so they lie about us. Those we lead might not want to do what it takes to follow our vision, so they look for greener (and easier) pastures at the first sign of a challenge. These situations are only the tip of the iceberg, but whatever the case, know that your responsibility is to fulfill God's mission, not to make your co-laborers happy and comfortable. It is He who gives you the vision, and He will help you carry it through, no matter how others treat you.

# Rejected by a Leader

The wounds you receive from a leader you highly esteem can send your world into a tailspin. Have you ever trusted a spiritual leader and then discovered that he or she was only using you for their purpose and never intended to develop your potential? How does a daughter of the King respond to this kind of rejection?

We can look at the story of one of our faith heroes—David —to discover the royal way to deal with rejection by a leader. First Samuel 16:14–18 describes the beginning of the relationship between a young David and his king, Saul.

> Now the Spirit of the Lord had departed from Saul, and an evil spirit from the Lord tormented him. Saul's attendants said to him, "See, an evil spirit from God is tormenting you. Let our lord command his servants here to search for someone who can play the harp. He will play when the evil spirit from God comes upon you, and you will feel better." So Saul said to his attendants, "Find someone who plays well and bring him to me." One of the servants answered, "I have seen a son of Jesse of Bethlehem who knows how to play the harp. He is a brave man and a warrior. He speaks well and is a fine-looking man. And the Lord is with him."

We discover from these verses that Saul initiated the relationship between himself and David in order to fill a personal need. David had the right set of skills, so he was chosen for the position in Saul's court. First Samuel 16:21 tells us, "David came to Saul and entered his service. Saul liked him very much, and David became one of his armor-bearers." Have you, like David, ever served under someone who needed your skills? Perhaps you truly respected that person and wanted to serve him or her with your whole heart, and you were excited to use any skill you had for that leader . . . but then the tide turned when God began using your skills to bless others besides your leader.

As God blesses you with success, there will be some leaders who will be excited to see your development and who will gladly encourage you to soar. However, there will also be those who will feel insecure, jealous, and threatened by your success because they never had your best interest in mind. Instead, they will only value you for what you can do for them. The sad news is that some leaders will only pour into your life as long as you serve their agenda and as long as they are recognized as being more successful than you are.

David knew what that was all about. First Samuel 18:5 says, "Whatever Saul sent him to do, David did it so successfully that Saul gave him a high rank in the army. This pleased all the people, and Saul's officers as well." But then the people started to honor David more than they honored Saul, and Saul didn't like it. Scripture tells us, "And from that time on Saul kept a jealous eye on David" (v. 9). Saul was so jealous of David that he tried to kill him (1 Samuel 18:10–11). When David was able to elude him, Saul became worried.

> Saul was afraid of David, because the Lord was with David but had left Saul. So he sent David away from him and gave him command over a thousand men, and David led the troops in their campaigns. In everything he did he had great success, because the Lord was with him. When Saul saw how successful he was, he was afraid of him. But all Israel and Judah loved David, because he led them in their campaigns. (1 Samuel 18:12–16)

The verses above show us that while our successes may cause a leader to reject us, they may also be a form of protection. Saul became afraid of David because David was so publicly successful. Saul left David alone for a while for fear of the crowds. However, he could not contain his jealousy and eventually decided that he needed to get rid of David. So David had to literally run for his life.

It would only seem natural that if someone is trying to harm you, and in the process you had the opportunity to harm them first, you would do it, right? That is the world's way, but that's not the way of the royal family. David had the chance to kill Saul, but he didn't take advantage of the opportunity. Saul and his army of three thousand men were out looking for David, and the following story unfolded:

> He came to the sheep pens along the way; a cave was there, and Saul went in to relieve himself. David and his men were far back in the cave. The men said, "This is the day the Lord spoke of when he said to you, 'I will give your enemy into your hands for you to deal with as you wish.'" Then David crept up unnoticed and cut off a corner of Saul's robe. Afterward, David was conscience-stricken for having cut off a corner of his robe. He said to his men, "The Lord forbid that I should do such a thing to my master, the Lord's anointed, or lift my hand against him; for he is the anointed of the Lord." With these words David rebuked his men and did not allow them to attack Saul. And Saul left the cave and went his way. (1 Samuel 24:3–7)

Not only did David not kill Saul when he had the chance, he even felt badly about cutting off part of his robe! Scripture tells us that after this, David approached Saul and let Saul know that he hadn't harmed him when he could have (v. 11). No matter how much someone has tried to harm you, the royal response is to attempt to make peace and to reconcile with the other person. However, there is no guarantee that the other person will want to reconcile. After David tried to reconcile, Saul again searched for David in order to kill him, and again, David had the opportunity to kill Saul but did not do so. David refused to take vengeance on Saul, and it meant

he had to spend the rest of Saul's life on the run. We read in
1 Samuel 27:1, "But David thought to himself, 'One of these
days I will be destroyed by the hand of Saul. The best thing I
can do is to escape to the land of the Philistines.'"

David did all he could to get along with Saul and to show
him that he meant him no harm. But time and time again,
Saul rejected David. When someone continues to reject you
to the point of seeking to destroy you, there comes a time
when you must decide to stop trying to reconcile. David had
to simply accept the rejection and move on. He made the
choice to stay out of Saul's way.

Saul's story does not have a happy ending. He and his sons
were in a battle with the Philistines, who killed his sons. Saul
himself was critically wounded, so Saul asked his armor-bearer
to finish killing him before the enemy could find him and tor-
ture him. When the armor-bearer refused, Saul fell on his own
sword, effectually ending his own life. At this point, you
would think David would be happy and relieved, wouldn't
you? But he wasn't. Scripture tells us how this royal man responded. "Then David and all the men with him took hold of
their clothes and tore them. They mourned and wept and
fasted till evening for Saul and his son Jonathan, and for the
army of the Lord and the house of Israel, because they had
fallen by the sword" (2 Samuel 1:11–12).

Just as David mourned for Saul, you may find yourself
grieving over a leader who has rejected you. Even when you
have been abandoned by someone, you still might feel deep
love for that person. No matter how you have been abused,
whether by a biological or spiritual leader, there is something
in a child's heart that longs for reconciliation with the parent.
We know the depth of our love when we find ourselves wanting forgiveness more than we want justice. We find ourselves
ready to forgive even when we aren't asked for forgiveness.
The sad truth is that some people will never ask for forgiveness. Instead of seeking peace, like Saul, they look for reasons

to stay divided. In cases such as these, it may be time to let go of the relationship and let God work out the end of the story.

The end of David's story is that he became a king who made mistakes, yet was a "man after [God's] own heart" (1 Samuel 13:14). Do you want to be a woman after God's own heart? Then follow the example of David when it comes to responding to a leader who has rejected you—keep your distance, forgive immediately and regularly, always have a heart that is open to restoration and friendship, and keep going to fulfill the mission God gave you.

## Rejected by Your Peers

It is not uncommon to find yourself rejected by your peers. This may happen when you're the new kid on the block, or it could be the result of success on your part that makes them feel threatened. Either way, the rejection hurts.

Joining an existing team can be tricky. You want to make a good impression and make a contribution, but at the same time, you might be afraid to share your ideas or vision for fear of ridicule, failure, or rejection. Even when an existing group is facing challenges and needing answers, it might take time for them to recognize God's answers through a newcomer. If God is doing a new thing, chances are that the person with the new vision will create a stir. God's vision often includes a readjustment in priorities, and you can be sure that the person who suggests these changes will face resistance.

The apostle Paul was a man who often created a stir. After his conversion, when he began to preach about Jesus, the other followers of Christ didn't immediately accept him. We read about this in Acts 9:26–31.

> When he came to Jerusalem, he tried to join the disciples, but they were all afraid of him, not believing that he really was a disciple. But Barnabas took him and brought him to

the apostles. He told them how Saul on his journey had seen the Lord and that the Lord had spoken to him, and how in Damascus he had preached fearlessly in the name of Jesus. So Saul stayed with them and moved about freely in Jerusalem, speaking boldly in the name of the Lord. He talked and debated with the Grecian Jews, but they tried to kill him. When the brothers learned of this, they took him down to Caesarea and sent him off to Tarsus. Then the church throughout Judea, Galilee and Samaria enjoyed a time of peace. It was strengthened; and encouraged by the Holy Spirit, it grew in numbers, living in the fear of the Lord.

Have you ever tried to fit in with an existing group only to have them look at you with suspicion? God gave Paul a vision for ministry and he "tried to join the disciples, but they were all afraid of him." The disciples only focused on part of Paul's background—the part where he had arrested Christians for their beliefs. They initially rejected him because they did not trust the vision God had given him. Is there something in your background that might cause others to be skeptical of you? Might your ethnicity, previous jobs, or personal issues from your past make others wary of listening to you and accepting your vision? When people reject you, it may be because of incomplete knowledge about you and about God's vision. However, if God is the one who sent you into a new group, then trust God to prove to the group that He appointed you for His mission.

In Paul's case, we see that God raised up Barnabas to introduce Paul to the apostles and explain the situation. After that, Paul was accepted and was able to go freely about the city, spreading the gospel message. Then we see again that another group rejected him, and even "tried to kill him." When the disciples heard of this, they promptly packed Paul up and shipped him out. Has something similar happened to you?

Have you created ripples that caused you to be sent away? If so, don't be too quick to label it as rejection. They may be sending you off because it is safer for you to be out of the picture for a season. They might accept your calling, yet question the timing. Consider that the issues surrounding you and the vision God gave you might be creating too much of a distraction at the moment and are hurting the programs that were working before you showed up on the scene.

Turning back to Paul's story, imagine what he was thinking when he heard through the grapevine that after he was sent away, the church in that area experienced a time of great peace and growth. How would you have felt? In our human flesh, we may hope that everything would crumble when we leave a place. We want to know that we made a difference and that we will be missed when we're gone—whether the leaving was on good or bad terms. But in God's plan, He may choose to bless the team or ministry that kicked us out the door. Scripture doesn't tell us what Paul did during his time in Tarsus, but based on what we know of the rest of his life, he most likely didn't sit around and feel sorry for himself. Paul's way was to serve wherever he was, no matter the circumstances.

We then see that in God's perfect timing, as His vision to reach the Gentiles matured, Paul entered the picture once again. "Then Barnabas went to Tarsus to look for Saul, and when he found him, he brought him to Antioch. So for a whole year Barnabas and Saul met with the church and taught great numbers of people" (Acts 11:25–26). God closed the door for Paul in Jerusalem, but He then opened one in Antioch. If you are in a place where your peers and colaborers do not value your contribution, receive it as God's open door for you to serve elsewhere. Know that if you were meant to continue in your current community, God will bring you back at a time when they will see you as an asset. Instead of licking your wounds and feeling rejected, know that no one can thwart God's plans. No one can ship you anywhere unless God allows it. Even in your exile, when you may feel isolated and forgotten, God is working His grand purpose.

## Rejected by Those You Lead

It is probably safe to say that there has never been a leader who hasn't been rejected by a follower. However, often the follower isn't actually rejecting the leader, but the leader's vision or the timeline of that vision. It sometimes seems as if people have God on a deadline. They will commit to following Him for six months, a year, or maybe even three years. But if the realization of the vision takes longer than they are willing to wait, they will wander off to follow a different dream.

When Moses accepted God's call to lead the children of Israel out of Egypt, he probably didn't expect the people to question his leadership every time they faced a challenge. If you have been entrusted with dreams that you are bringing to reality for a family, business, church, ministry, community, or nation, you need to learn to manage your expectations. No matter how much the people may praise you at the beginning, rest assured that some of them will have a low tolerance level for you and the vision once challenges come along. When the challenges mount past the point of their tolerance, be prepared for them to try to throw you out. It matters little how much you have endured, how much you have sacrificed, and how long you have served. Yesterday's miracles will be forgotten. People will make decisions based on what you have done (or not done) for them today.

Moses experienced this time and time again. Let's take a look at one of those times. When the Israelites arrived at the edge of the Promised Land, Moses sent scouts to survey the land. They returned with the following report: "We went into the land to which you sent us, and it does flow with milk and honey! Here is its fruit. But the people who live there are powerful, and the cities are fortified and very large. We even saw descendants of Anak there. . . . We can't attack those people; they are stronger than we are" (Numbers 13:27–28, 31). Often, people aren't pleased when they discover that it will take more than they expected to fulfill the vision or win the victory. They might not be willing to put in the extra hours, exhaust their resources, and accept the losses and risks that are associated with the mission. Anytime a situation calls for people to exhibit a greater level of faith than they are used to, you can be sure that most people will question their ability or desire to be a part of it.

Even if many of your followers reject the mission, there may still be those who are willing to take on the challenges. Moses found this in Caleb and Joshua. After returning from the surveying trip, they stood up to the others and said, "The land we passed through and explored is exceedingly good. If the Lord is pleased with us, he will lead us into that land, a land flowing with milk and honey, and will give it to us" (Numbers 14:7–8). Praise God when He raises up Calebs and Joshuas for you and your mission! You will need those sons and daughters of the King during the times when the rest of the people don't have the faith to keep going. But even if nobody will stand with you, know that God expects His leader to keep going forward with the vision. In the times when no one believes, the leader must have the faith to believe for the whole community.

The sad truth is that when the people rise up against God's leader, not only do the people pay the price, but the leader may have to pay it with them. Moses did.

The Lord said to Moses and Aaron: "How long will this wicked community grumble against me? I have heard the complaints of these grumbling Israelites. So tell them, 'As surely as I live, declares the Lord, I will do to you the very things I heard you say: In this desert your bodies will fall . . .

except Caleb son of Jephunneh and Joshua son of Nun. . . . For forty years—one year for each of the forty days you explored the land—you will suffer for your sins and know what it is like to have me against you.' I, the Lord, have spoken, and I will surely do these things to this whole wicked community, which has banded together against me. They will meet their end in this desert; here they will die." (Numbers 14:26–30, 34–35)

Not only did Moses have to wander with the people for forty years, but we also read that at the end, Moses struck out in anger against the people and was also banned from entering the Promised Land (Numbers 20:12). Had the people not grumbled against the Lord, Moses would have been able to lead the people into that land flowing with milk and honey. Instead, he died in the wilderness, and Joshua was charged with the mission to lead the people into the Promised Land.

In the ministry of Inspire Women, God has taught me that even when the mission is delayed by those who lack faith, that doesn't give me the right to say to Him, "Well, I led them to the edge of the Promised Land. If they don't have the faith to enter, that shouldn't impact my life." In those situations, I have tried to convince God that He should release me or that I have finished His assignment. But God has shown me in His Word that when the people will not follow His leader, it will delay the timing for everyone to reach God's intended end. I learned that I do not have the freedom to give God a deadline. I don't get to say, "God, You have one year to finish this assignment or I'm leaving!"

God called Moses to lead the children of Israel into the Promised Land. Even though Moses didn't physically make it, before he died, he passed the mantle on to Joshua. God doesn't change His mission. If God gave you the specifics for a mission, know that God's leader is entrusted with the mission until it is accomplished.

# How God Showed Me
# His Power through My Son

When my son, Robbie, turned twenty-one, I found myself reflecting back on key events in his life. I recalled an incident from his elementary school years that could have permanently affected his image of himself.

Robbie was always confident of his ability to make good presentations at school. For one particular assignment, he went to the extra work of making a costume to wear for his presentation in order to earn bonus points. When I picked him up from school that day, he was visibly upset. When I asked him what happened, he said, "The teacher hated my presentation. She took points off for the costume I made. That was supposed to be for bonus points. I have never heard of a teacher who took away points for the extra work you did to get bonus points!"

That night, while Robbie was asleep, I went into his room, placed my head on his chest while he was sleeping, and poured out prayers on his behalf. I begged God to protect him and not to allow this teacher's rejection of his work to hurt him and make him question his gifts and abilities. I was so intense in my prayers that I began to heave and weep. Robbie woke up in a panic over my emotions. He said, "Mom, what's wrong? Did someone die?" I said, "No, Son. I was just so devastated over what your teacher did to you. I don't want you to believe her opinion. I don't want her to rob you of the gift God placed in you." I was relieved by his response: "Mom, don't worry. I don't care what this teacher says. She doesn't have that kind of power over me."

Robbie was only eleven when he formed this conclusion, but his words have stayed with me through the years. I remember them when I am in similar situations. I wonder if you have given the power to redefine your life in negative ways to someone who has no authority to do so. The truth is that

God is the one who deposited gifts in us, He is pleased with what He has created, and He is the only one who should have power over us. May His approval of our service be all that we need to keep going in the face of rejection.

# Chapter 8

# *When Your*

## CALLING
## IS REJECTED

"Therefore . . . stand firm. Let
nothing move you."

1 Corinthians 15:58

Sometimes when God calls us, He calls us
to something unique, something different,
something new. And other times His calling is for us to
do the same thing that many others have done
throughout the centuries. But no matter what He calls
us to do, we can expect God's calling to require faith.
If we are doing God's will, we can also rest assured
that Satan won't leave us alone; he will do his best to
try to keep us from the Lord's work. In the midst of
God stretching our faith, the devil will often use others to try to convince us that what we heard wasn't a
call at all. There will be people who will reject our calling, but we must stand firm. Even when people don't
understand, affirm, or accept our calling, it is our responsibility to keep doing what God has called us to do.

Sometimes we might even find ourselves rejecting
someone else's calling. When that happens, consider
your motives and try to give others the freedom to

hear God's voice for themselves. The challenge is for all of us to respect each other's callings and trust that God can and will lead each of us in His own way in order to fulfill His purposes for the whole world. Don't make the mistake of thinking that your calling is everyone else's calling. God uses various people, methods, and resources to carry out His vision. Ultimately, we all answer to Him. He has commissioned us to take His Word to the ends of the earth, and nothing should stop us from carrying out that mission.

## Designed to Be a Blessing

When God's Word is proclaimed, it is designed to be a blessing to its hearers. But that doesn't necessarily mean that people will listen to it. Jesus experienced this with the Pharisees in Luke 13:34–35:

> O Jerusalem, Jerusalem, you who kill the prophets and stone those sent to you, how often I have longed to gather your children together, as a hen gathers her chicks under her wings, but you were not willing! Look, your house is left to you desolate. I tell you, you will not see me again until you say, "Blessed is he who comes in the name of the Lord."

Jesus did not allow the critical spirit of those who didn't like His message to keep Him from fulfilling God's call on His life. He focused on what His message was intended to do for the people. He did not allow their response to dampen His passion because He stayed connected to God's original intentions.

The message Jesus brought was meant to be a blessing. But it is also clear that even when your motives are right and your message was designed to be a blessing, there is no guarantee that the audience will receive you kindly. The fact is that those who come to hear us often process our message through the lens of their own personal agendas. What we say may threaten their turf, as it did with Jesus and the Pharisees. When we represent God's message, we need to manage our expectations and realize that God often speaks words that will require others to adjust their priorities. What we say, therefore, may threaten someone's resources, their career plans, or their own aspirations for where they were heading in business or ministry. It's not our fault when God's message challenges someone's personal agenda. But the fact is that they will take it out on the message bearer.

If you have been criticized for your message, consider whether your message was designed to bless. Is it truly the Word of God? Are you following the path God laid down for you? If so, then focus on the fact that you were designed to be a blessing, and keep blessing no matter what people think. Don't apologize for your calling or your message, but stay in the blessing of what God has called you to do and say.

## Trust God with the Outcome

Sometimes our response to the criticism of our calling and message should be to walk away. But other times, God might lead us to keep ministering to those same people. Aggressive action, instead of retreat, may well be part of His plan. It was definitely the plan for one of our faith heroes, Stephen. Acts 7:54–60 tells us what happened to Stephen when he faced criticism and his calling was rejected by the religious leaders of the day.

When they heard this, they were furious and gnashed their teeth at him. But Stephen, full of the Holy Spirit, looked up to heaven and saw the glory of God, and Jesus standing at the right hand of God. "Look," he said, "I see heaven open and the Son of Man standing at the right hand of

God." At this they covered their ears and, yelling at the top of their voices, they all rushed at him, dragged him out of the city and began to stone him. Meanwhile, the witnesses laid their clothes at the feet of a young man named Saul. While they were stoning him, Stephen prayed, "Lord Jesus, receive my spirit." Then he fell on his knees and cried out, "Lord, do not hold this sin against them." When he had said this, he fell asleep.

This account of Stephen's stoning shows us that the critical spirit in others could cause them to take action against us. Yet, in spite of this, Stephen never questioned whether he was to speak out. He did not demand God's protection. He trusted in God's decision to do with the situation as He willed. All he was focused on was the content of his message and his certainty that he was in God's timetable.

If we judge situations by their outcomes, we might find ourselves saying, "Stephen, maybe you should have been more diplomatic. Maybe you should have won your audience over before you shared so many facts. You didn't have to lie, but maybe you shouldn't have revealed all the truth." But Stephen was sure of his content and his timing because God's Word tells us that he was "full of the Holy Spirit." When you know your heart is connected with God's heart, message, and timing, then no matter what criticism is directed against you, keep going! If the outcome turns out in such a way that you get thrown out or your mission is killed, trust that what happens next will fit into God's overall plan.

Observe that Stephen didn't have any kind of personal crisis. He did not say, "God, how could You have allowed this to happen? Here I was doing the very thing You asked me to do. If You are in this, why am I about to be killed?" Up until the very end, Stephen kept his mission pure by keeping his heart connected with God's heart. God sent him with a message to bless the people, so Stephen stayed true to being a blessing until his very last breath. He appealed to the Lord not to hold the people's misguided actions against them.

Have you allowed yourself to be resentful of those who are critical of you? Have you found yourself striking out at them instead of forgiving them? Have you wished for God to judge them and for them to get what they deserve when they stand before Him instead of appealing to God for their forgiveness? When we focus on being the blessing God intended us to be, then no matter how anyone reacts, we find our strength by staying on course.

Let's take one last look at the outcome of Stephen's stand for Christ and His message. Scripture tells us what happened directly after Stephen's death in Acts 8:1. "On that day a great persecution broke out against the church at Jerusalem, and all except the apostles were scattered throughout Judea and Samaria." At first glance, this would seem to be a very bad thing. Almost all of Christ's followers fled Jerusalem and were scattered, which meant they could no longer meet together and worship the Lord. But on the other hand, this scattering meant that Christ's message was spread through these persecuted people to many places throughout the land. If they had all stayed in Jerusalem, it would have taken much longer for the message to be taken to others. Stephen died, but the message spread. Stephen trusted God with the outcome, and what an outcome it was!

## Keep Obeying Even When You Look Foolish

There are times when God allows us to be in a place where we become the target of the public's criticism, but through it all, He expects us to keep going . . . to keep obeying, even if we look foolish. We can find an example of this in our royal family tree, with the best-known woman in the Bible —Mary. Remember that our royal family has a royal code of behavior. When we model our lives after the correct behavior of our faith heroes, we affirm our identity as the royal daughter of the King.

You know the story of Mary—how God chose her to be the mother of His Son Jesus. But let's look at it in light of the subject at hand—keeping on course even when our sense of calling is criticized or rejected. We read the angel's proclamation to Mary in Luke 1:30–33.

> Do not be afraid, Mary, you have found favor with God. You will be with child and give birth to a son, and you are to give him the name Jesus. He will be great and will be called the Son of the Most High. The Lord God will give him the throne of his father David, and he will reign over the house of Jacob forever; his kingdom will never end.

Sounds great, right? Well, not so fast. Mary wasn't yet married, but she was going to have a child. In light of her culture, she would have reason to be scared. God was putting her into a situation where she was bound to be the target of everyone's criticism. To make matters more complicated, what could Mary say to defend herself that wouldn't make matters worse? How would people take the information that she was called to be the mother of the Messiah? Such a claim would sound arrogant and would evoke further criticism: "Who do you think you are to think that God would appoint you to such a privileged place?"

But we see that Mary did not dwell on fear or on what people would say. Instead, she focused on the awesomeness of God's appointment and said, "My soul glorifies the Lord and my spirit rejoices in God my Savior, for he has been mindful of the humble state of his servant. From now on all generations will call me blessed, for the Mighty One has done great things for me—holy is his name" (Luke 1:46–49). In spite of the criticism that was sure to come, Mary clung to the fact that God had "done great things" for her.

Mary could have said, "You know, God, I'm going to look awfully silly." I've been in that situation before. When I left the College of Biblical Studies to launch Inspire Women as an independent organization, I drove away from campus with my car full of boxes and nowhere to go. My new ministry was completely homeless, and I knew some people felt I had made a stupid decision. I wish I could say that I left boldly, but I didn't. I left with tears streaming down my face. And I felt kind of silly. Have you ever felt that way? To look at another story from our royal family, I imagine that Noah probably had times that he felt silly when he was building the ark. He was building a huge boat when there wasn't any rain, and you can imagine how ridiculous he must have felt while his neighbors watched incredulously. But Noah persevered. The fact of the matter is that God doesn't care how silly we look to others.

God had to teach me to keep obeying even if I looked like a fool. I learned how to discern God's favor from Mary's example. She must have felt the public ridicule as she walked around unwed and pregnant. In a similar way, I felt the derision of those who saw me walking around with a ministry that was homeless. Neither situation was something that you would want to broadcast to the world.

I wondered if Mary wished her pregnancy could be over with quickly so God would announce the Messiah and show the world that her condition was necessary for what He was birthing. I felt like I was carrying the ministry of Inspire Women in my womb, but before God established it, I would experience the ridicule of those around me. No one understood how crazy I felt to drive away from an established institution to build something with no resources.

How do we endure an embarrassing situation that is part of God's plan? The only way is when we know God's Word and therefore can discern His timing and favor in the midst of what appears to the public eye to be a bad situation.

Mary did not go down in history as an unwed mother. Even though God allowed the criticism for a season, He made sure the ones who really needed to see God's truth were given the Truth. God made sure the angel also appeared to Joseph so Mary would have the support she needed. Similarly, in spite of the criticism I encountered, God opened the eyes of those He handpicked to support me as I carried out God's mission for His daughters in Houston. No human manipulation or criticism can keep God's plans from going forward. The next time you face criticism, learn to focus on where God is going. The greater plan will silence the noise around you and help you to stay focused in spite of rejection.

## Be Radical

Rejection won't just come when you do something that seems silly or foolish, but also when you're being radical for Christ. There will always be people who will tell you to lead a more balanced life. But that isn't the way our royal family does things. Take Paul, for example. There was nothing balanced about his life. He did things to the extreme. Take a look at what he says in 2 Corinthians 11:23–28:

> I have worked much harder, been in prison more frequently, been flogged more severely, and been exposed to death again and again. Five times I received from the Jews the forty lashes minus one. Three times I was beaten with rods, once I was stoned, three times I was shipwrecked, I spent a night and a day in the open sea, I have been constantly on the move. I have been in danger from rivers, in danger from bandits, in danger from my own countrymen, in danger from Gentiles; in danger in the city, in danger in the country, in danger at sea; and in danger from false brothers. I have labored and toiled and have often gone without sleep; I have known hunger and thirst and have

often gone without food; I have been cold and naked. Besides everything else, I face daily the pressure of my concern for all the churches.

Don't be surprised when you find people rejecting you for your momentum. They will accuse you of tiring them out. Instead of encouraging you, they will avoid you. Rest assured that there were those who ran from Paul as well. Not everyone is comfortable being in the midst of those who are radical for God or who are called to run at a different pace.

Not everyone is called to live to the extremes like Paul was. Some are called to lead a movement, some are called to lead a church, some to lead a company, others to lead a family, some to lead a few individuals, and a rare few who are called to lead all of the above. So don't feel guilty if you don't move at the pace of Paul. You must simply settle in your heart what God has entrusted you to finish. And if it takes extreme living to get there, then go for it, despite any criticism or rejection you might face.

The important thing to think about is how you will feel about your life the day your time on earth is over. Will you want to be remembered as someone who was lukewarm or someone who was radical—someone who did whatever she needed to do to fulfill God's purpose? In Revelation 3:16, God says, "So, because you are lukewarm—neither hot nor cold—I am about to spit you out of my mouth." It is tempting to be lukewarm. Thoughts of shopping all day, sitting by the pool, and lunching with friends sound really good. Those aren't necessarily bad things to do on occasion, but beware of letting them overshadow your work for the Lord.

I often hear people criticizing those who are passionate for God, and suggesting they be more moderate. But what is strange about this is that often this counsel for moderation only applies to God's projects. It's rare to hear people advising businesspeople in the secular world to be less radical or extreme. Those who spend a great amount of time and energy building a financial empire, starting a new business from scratch, or fighting for our country are applauded for their work, not criticized. But when it comes to starting ministries and expanding God's kingdom into enemy territory, we seem to have a double standard. My heart breaks for the leaders who are criticized for doing what is necessary to advance God's mission, because that criticism is based in deception. The devil enjoys convincing us that our lives are off balance when we work hard for God, but that it is perfectly fine to work at an insane pace in the secular world. This is not to say that our families should be neglected for the sake of the call. God expects us to fulfill our roles within our family. But that doesn't mean we can't be radical for Him outside our homes, too.

Don't buy into the lie that we should regulate our work for the Lord. God's work is not a hobby that we fit into our lives with moderation. As a matter of fact, it is the only activity that will count in eternity.

## How God Helped Me Triumph over Criticism

Did you know that the number one fear in adults is the fear of public speaking? This fear is likely based on other fears—the fear of failure and the fear of criticism. Think about it for a moment. After you hear a speaker, how often do you find something to criticize in what he or she had to say?

Even though I speak in front of crowds on a consistent basis, I still occasionally find myself in a state of panic. I recall one time in particular when my entire speech was nearly derailed. Usually when I speak on a large stage, the bright lights shining in my eyes keep me from seeing the faces of the people in the audience. But one night when I was sharing the story of my personal journey, the lights were different and I could see the faces of the women in the crowd. Halfway through my talk, I froze and couldn't remember what to say next. For a moment, there was absolute silence.

I frantically prayed and said to God, "If You don't rescue me, I'm just going to stand here and say nothing." I could literally feel God rescue me, and I finished the talk as if nothing had happened. But I knew something *had* happened, and I needed to get to the bottom of the problem so it wouldn't happen again. So I said to the Lord, "Examine my heart, God, and show me what happened tonight!"

God took me back to the exact moment when I froze. It was when I looked into the eyes of one of the women sitting in the front row; I could see her critical spirit. Was it my hair? My clothes? My ethnic background? My way of speaking? What was she criticizing? I didn't know what it was, but there was something about me that made her reject me as a speaker; something made her reject my calling to invest my time in inspiring and training women. I had to face my own insecurities and take a hard look at my need to be accepted by others. And God showed me that He and I had conflicting goals.

God did not send me into that crowd to get their acceptance or to win a popularity contest. I wasn't there to win their votes. Instead, God sent me to redirect their focus onto His plans for the world. I had to decide whether my purpose was to win the crowd's approval or if it was to inspire those around me to be on the same page with God. I chose the latter. What I learned is this: Once we settle in our hearts that life is about God, then He is the one on stage. We are simply His mouthpiece.

# Section 3

## *Transforming Fear*

### TO FULFILL GOD'S PURPOSE

WHEN JESUS WAS CARRYING the cross on the way to Calvary, Mark tells us, "A certain man from Cyrene, Simon, the father of Alexander and Rufus, was passing by on his way in from the country, and they forced him to carry the cross" (Mark 15:21). This man, Simon, was simply minding his own business when all of a sudden he was forced into a service he didn't ask for and that he most likely didn't want.

Has something like that ever happened to you? Most of us will find that at some point in our lives, we will be "passing by," doing our own thing, when God intersects our lives with a divine agenda. When the invitation first shows up on our radar screen, we are caught unaware because our minds were focused on other things. Then as we get pulled into it, we think, "How did I get involved in this? Why am I here? How do I get this over with so I can get back to what I was doing?"

Imagine the scene Simon was pulled into. There was a major mob of activity around Jesus. Unfriendly Roman guards were everywhere, protecting their prisoner. They had swords. They had a commanding presence and demanded the utmost allegiance of those around them.

To have one of them look your way would strike fear in your heart. And to have one of them command you to walk beside the very person they were executing was probably not a job for which you would have volunteered. Touching the cross, and perhaps touching the one who was to be killed—his bloody skin, his filthy clothes—was not a job anyone would choose. But that is the job that was forced upon Simon.

Fast-forward a minute to the future. What do we know about this Simon of Cyrene? Mark told us he was "the father of Alexander and Rufus." Mark must have known that his readers would know of these men. In fact, this Rufus was likely the same one Paul mentioned in Romans 16:13, "Greet Rufus, chosen in the Lord, and his mother, who has been a mother to me, too." If this was the case, then he (and probably his brother as well) was a prominent leader in the early church. With this in mind, consider that Simon's encounter with God could have transformed not only his own life, but the lives of his children and the lives of the people his children led.

God's Word tells us that in Simon's case, "they forced him to carry the cross." The "they" in this story were the Roman guards who represented a secular force. Has God used a secular system to force you in a direction you didn't want to go? Perhaps your company pushed you into early retirement. Maybe you were laid off from your job. You might feel helpless in the very circumstances that God used to put you exactly where He wanted you to be. While you think you're in the wrong place at the wrong time, God is thinking, "You are right on time!"

In God's grace, He allows circumstances to force our footsteps not because He is trying to take something away from us but because He desires to give us more. If you feel pressured by your situation, instead of getting mad or fearful, try changing your paradigm to think of it this way: our human minds are often too short-sighted to see the blessings God puts in front of us. So praise God for the pressure, because sometimes that pressure is necessary to get us on the same page with God.

The next time you find yourself shrinking from a new opportunity, ask yourself if you are missing a divine appointment because you are allowing your dread of the situation to cloud your vision. Are you concerned with what the assignment will require from you personally? You may need to stop and ask, "Where was I on my way to? Is what I was doing as critical as what God has redirected my time, my energy, or my resources to do?" It is so incredible how God works. His plans always give us more than we could ever imagine for ourselves. Remember that Alexander and Rufus were affected eternally because their father was forced to be part of God's agenda. At the time, there was no way Simon could have known the results of his encounter with Jesus.

Pastor Leonard Barksdale, a former attorney who God called to serve as a pastor in a low-income neighborhood, once said to me, "Remember, Anita, that Simon only got to help carry the cross, but Jesus was the one who went all the way to Calvary." Those were comforting words at a time when God's call on my life felt daunting. From his counsel, I was reminded that God is the one who has paid the price for His own dreams. He's not putting the weight of the world on our shoulders. He carries the world. He is the Savior. What he invites us to do is to be part of the journey.

As the guardian of dreams for yourself, your family, your business, your church, your ministry, your community, your nation, or the world, have you allowed your fears to cause you to abandon what God intended to do through you? Fear is not from God. In God's perfect love, there is no fear.

In this third and final section, I will share with you how God taught me to stay focused on His mission in spite of fear. We will look at God's truth to rise above fear when you face suffering, when you fear failure, when you fear loss, and when you are affected by the choices of others, among other situations.

Like we've done before, as daughters of the King of Kings, we will look at how the faith heroes in our royal family tree dealt with the emotion of fear in the events of their lives. Through their example, we will discover the royal family's code of behavior. I praise God for those role models who have gone before us and finished well.

We don't get to pass this way again. In the time that we have, we can't control how we feel, but we can choose to allow God to harness our emotions and transform them into a passionate purpose to fulfill His dreams.

# Chapter 9

## *When You*

### FACE
### SUFFERING

"Yet not as I will, but as you will."

Matthew 26:39

Over the years, I have often heard people teach that the sole purpose of humankind is to glorify God. Those words always sounded spiritual to me, but since I had no idea what the word "glorify" meant, I didn't know how I was supposed to glorify God. Then I learned that when you glorify something you convey its importance. So therefore God will be glorified when we show the world how important He is by the choices we make.

In our human minds we may want to think of glorifying God in terms of writing a best seller, drawing a crowd of thousands to hear us speak, or simply being successful so that He will look good. However, a more accurate description of glorifying God may be taking the opportunity to show the world how important God is by our willingness to suffer or to sacrifice for Him. In fact, the more difficult the challenge we endure for Christ's sake, the louder the message we send to the world of how worthy of our suffering our God is.

On the night Jesus was arrested, He said, "Father, the time has come. Glorify your Son, that your Son may glorify you" (John 17:1). Jesus knew what was coming, yet He recognized that the suffering He would endure was His greatest opportunity to glorify God. Is this how you view suffering in your life? When God trusts you with His dreams, know that suffering will be a part of it, just as it was with Jesus. As God conforms us to the image of His Son, we cannot avoid suffering as part of our journey. It's not a question of whether you will ever suffer; it is more a question of how you will respond when suffering enters your life. It is not unspiritual to fear suffering, but it is un-Christlike to fear it to the point of trying to avoid it when God trusts you with a cross of your own.

## As God Wills

Was Jesus terrified of the cross? We know that He was not oblivious of the facts. He knew what it would take to go to the cross. He knew what it meant to have the sins of the world put on His shoulders. Even though He was blameless, He was going to death row for all humankind. Worse still, He knew that for a moment in time, the entire wrath of God would be poured out on Him. Can you imagine God redirecting all of His wrath to you alone?

So how did Jesus get past any fear so that He could fulfill the mission God had given Him? We read this prayer in Matthew 26:39: "My Father, if it is possible, may this cup be taken from me. Yet not as I will, but as you will." Don't miss the fact that it was the relationship between Jesus and His Father that settled the question of whether He would go to the cross. If you wonder whether you could do the same, think of it this way. Are there people in your life that you would suffer and sacrifice more for than others? And when you do choose to suffer or sacrifice on another's behalf, is it not your relationship with them that causes you to decide what you will bear for them? In Jesus' case, it was His relationship with His Father that got Him past the fear to obedience. Once Jesus was sure of what His Father wanted Him to do, His answer was, "Yes."

Jesus knew how much His Father loved Him, and He knew that God would never have asked Him to go to the cross if there had been another option. But the only solution that would satisfy God's characteristics of justice and love was for Him to give up His one and only Son to appease the law's penalty of death for sin and to fully exhibit His love for us by sending His Son to pay that penalty. Jesus knew how deep His relationship was with His Father, and that is what gave Jesus the ability to sacrifice for Him. Is your relationship with God that deep? If there is something that you are unwilling to do for God because of your fear of suffering or sacrifice, it is because your relationship with Him is not deep enough.

We will find our peace when we trust our relationship with our Father to the point that we freely give what He asks as soon as we are sure it is something He desires. Jesus knew why God had called Him to die on the cross. But even when we don't know why, we should still be willing to sacrifice for God. When God called me to establish Inspire Women, I didn't understand why. The only question I asked was, "Father, do You want this?" As soon as I heard in my spirit that it was something He wanted, I had my marching orders. I knew that whatever it took and however long it took, I was to keep giving God what His heart longed for.

Once Jesus was sure of God's will, He no longer wrestled with God's decision for Him to suffer. Matthew 26:45–46 tells us what happened right after Jesus submitted to the Father's will. "Then he returned to the disciples and said to them, 'Are you still sleeping and resting? Look, the hour is near, and the Son of Man is betrayed into the hands of sinners. Rise, let us go! Here comes my betrayer!'" The moment had arrived, and Jesus literally walked right into God's divine appointment. He could have run the other way. No one could have forced Jesus to go to the cross. Even the nails couldn't have kept Him there if He had decided to leave. But Jesus knew what had to happen. When Peter tried to physically defend Jesus and block His arrest, Jesus said to him: "Put your sword back in its place . . . for all who draw the sword will die by the sword. Do you think I cannot call on my Father, and he will at once put at my disposal more than twelve legions of angels? But how then would the Scriptures be fulfilled that say it must happen this way?" (Matthew 26:52–54). From Jesus' example, we learn that the desire to obey God must be greater than any fear.

It is one thing to say, "Yes," with our mouths, but it is quite another thing to do "Yes" with our lives. How did Jesus fulfill His commitment to God? It was His trust in His Father's heart. He knew God wasn't leading Him to Calvary to leave Him there. He recognized that God would lead Him past Calvary to the resurrection. God does the same for us. There is no value in suffering for the sake of suffering. God allows suffering because of what it accomplishes. We already know what Jesus accomplished for us on the cross. And not only did Jesus die for our sins, He is also our greatest faith hero.

Jesus set the royal family standard when He allowed Himself to be hung on the cross. Hebrews 12:2–3 tells us: "Let us fix our eyes on Jesus, the author and perfecter of our faith, who for the joy set before him endured the cross, scorning its shame, and sat down at the right hand of the throne of God. Consider him who endured such opposition from sinful men, so that you will not grow weary and lose heart." Jesus focused on the victory that would come after the suffering. It is the joy that follows the cross that will carry us through, as well.

## We Are Not Alone in Our Suffering

We often think that our sufferings are unique—that we are the only ones going through tough times. But the fact is that we are not alone. Everyone suffers. We don't necessarily suffer in the same ways, yet we all experience suffering. First Peter 5:8–9 declares this to be true. "Be self-controlled and alert. Your enemy the devil prowls around like a roaring lion looking for someone to devour. Resist him, standing firm in the faith, because you know that your brothers throughout the world are undergoing the same kind of sufferings." Anyone called to represent Christ will have a cross to bear.

You may not always be able to see what someone else's cross is, but you can be sure that everyone has one. If you come from a background of abuse, your cross may consist of walking back into situations of abuse to minister to others who are being abused. Or perhaps your cross may include having to work through your own memories and continuously having to claim God's victory over wounds from the past that have been reopened. But we do not have the luxury of picking out our own cross. God is the one who chooses the stage on which He will display His power. Satan tries to discourage us by causing us to compare our crosses to someone else and thinking ours is harder to bear. But all believers go through "the same kind of sufferings," though they may appear in different forms.

## Stand Firm in the Silence

As we face unknown challenges and suffering, we feel we need God's presence more than anything else. Yet, for some reason, we often find Him to be silent during those times. Moses experienced this same thing. When he was treading in unknown territory, he said to the Lord, "If your Presence does not go with us, do not send us up from here. How will anyone know that you are pleased with me and with your people unless you go with us? What else will distinguish me and your people from all the other people on the face of the earth?" (Exodus 33:15–16). Moses wanted God's presence as he faced the unknown.

Jesus also knew what it was like to feel the absence of God's presence. His ultimate test of faith was when He experienced God's silence as He hung on the cross. "From the sixth hour until the ninth hour darkness came over all the land. About the ninth hour Jesus cried out in a loud voice, . . . 'My God, my God, why have you forsaken me?'" (Matthew 27:45–46). Jesus experienced darkness that we will never know. Yet we can gather from His story that since even Jesus wasn't exempt from God's silence during the hardest time in His life, neither will we be. However, knowing this ahead of time prepares us for the challenge. And we know that God will not remain silent, as was the case for Jesus.

Jesus' death on the cross did not end with abandonment but with His resurrection. God was silent for a time, but then He rescued His own. Jesus knew that when the time came for Him to die, God would be there to receive Him, and He was. That's why He was able to state in Luke 23:46, "Father, into your hands I commit my spirit." Think about it. How can you commit your spirit into the hands of a God who is absent? Committing His spirit was an act of faith.

Following Jesus' example, we must also trust God in the midst of our suffering, no matter how silent He may be. We must trust that God will break the silence and stay true to His character. Psalm 72:12–14 tells us, "For he will deliver the needy who cry out, the afflicted who have no one to help. He will take pity on the weak and the needy and save the needy from death. He will rescue them from oppression and violence, for precious is their blood in his sight." While we know that God will choose our cross, we also know that He will choose how He will deliver us from it . . . and that deliverance may not come on this earth. Many have sacrificed their lives for the sake of God's call, but their deaths do not mean that God didn't care about them. Because Jesus stayed on that cross and rose from the grave, we have the assurance that when we leave this earth, we will be eternally delivered from suffering.

There will be seasons when you won't sense God's presence in the midst of your suffering. However, instead of being afraid, recognize your situation as an opportunity to become more like Jesus. Like Jesus, we must trust that whatever suffering God allows to touch our lives will be for the fulfillment of a greater plan. Therefore, we need to choose ahead of time —even before the pillars of our lives start to shake—that we will not be shaken. We can rejoice that God deemed us worthy to share in the fellowship of His Son's suffering by giving us a situation where we have the chance to trust Him like Jesus did. In spite of God's silence, we can step into our identities as members of God's royal family tree and show the world how royalty responds to a cross.

## Focus on God, Not the Enemy

Not all suffering comes as a result of following God's call. If you are experiencing physical, emotional, or sexual abuse, know that God is not glorified by that suffering. However, He can be glorified in the way you remove yourself from a setting that dishonors what God would want for His daughter. When your physical welfare is at risk, you may need to do everything you can to get out of the situation. You cannot focus on God's mission when you are continuously in survival mode in a threatening environment.

If you are in a situation where you fear for your physical welfare but nothing has happened yet, follow David's example and trust in God's power. "When evil men advance against me to devour my flesh, when my enemies and my foes attack me, they will stumble and fall. Though an army besiege me, my heart will not fear; though war break out against me, even then will I be confident" (Psalm 27:2–3). How did David get to a place where he would not give in to fear? The next verse explains it. "One thing I ask of the Lord, this is what I seek: that I may dwell in the house of the Lord all the days of my life, to gaze upon the beauty of the Lord and to seek him in his temple" (Psalm 27:4).

David sought to fill his mind with God's reality, and so must we. Whenever we allow people or situations to frighten us, we are focusing too much on the enemy and we need to redirect our focus to God. If your personal sanctuary has been invaded, allow yourself to be transported in your mind and soul to God's sanctuary. Visualize God sitting on His throne with Jesus at His right hand. Imagine the angels singing and praising God. Remember Jesus' words in Matthew 28:18: "All authority in heaven and on earth has been given to me." Instead of focusing on the evil around you, focus on God's power to overcome evil.

This authority Jesus speaks of was mentioned in the context of the Great Commission—sharing God's message throughout the earth. "Therefore go and make disciples of all nations, baptizing them in the name of the Father and of the Son and of the Holy Spirit, and teaching them to obey everything I have commanded you. And surely I am with you always, to the very end of the age" (Matthew 28:19–20). Jesus said He would be with us always. The best way to experience His presence and protection is for us to be about God's business.

Jesus is sending us to the ends of the earth with His full authority and presence. Instead of hiding in fear, it is time for us to make disciples of all nations by sharing the message that God came to earth through His Son. He offers us the gift of forgiveness and eternal life. Moreover, when we accept His gift and become part of the royal family, He gives us His power to represent Him and proclaim His name on earth.

We are not victims; we were designed to be conquerors. We are warriors of the King of Kings, and God is sending us into our communities to transform the world with God's power. When we enter any environment, we are to represent our Father's heart. We are to look at things with our Father's eyes. When we leave a neighborhood, a workplace, or a community, something should have changed as evidence that God's daughter visited this place.

Choosing to overcome fear for your physical well-being by trusting in God's power does not mean that you should just blindly walk into abusive circumstances, however. If you are in a situation where you are being threatened physically, know that God has authority over your situation and that He does not want you to live in such circumstances. Therefore, exercise authority in your heavenly Father's name and take action to move to safer ground instead of just allowing others to hurt you. If you are unable to get out safely, then pray and ask God for an escape plan. The courage to leave comes from knowing that all authority in heaven and earth has been given to Jesus, and He has commissioned us to represent Him in the world. So we are to step into our appointment with confidence. We are to say, "No more," to situations that God would never bless. We need to declare, "Something must change," about situations that grieve God's heart. And we also need to consider that perhaps God has allowed us to experience threats to our physical welfare because He wants us to strengthen our faith before He sends us in His name to change a similar situation in another place.

## We Are Soldiers in God's Army

When we represent God's heart of justice and mercy, we become an active member of God's army. The apostle Paul did not skip a beat in spite of countless attacks on his physical body. He was not surprised by any assault that was directed at him. He kept going in spite of every physical injury. Look at the list of dangers he faced:

Three times I was beaten with rods, once I was stoned, three times I was shipwrecked, I spent a night and a day in the open sea, I have been constantly on the move. I have been in danger from rivers, in danger from bandits, in danger from my own countrymen, in danger from Gentiles; in danger in the city, in danger in the country, in danger at sea; and in danger from false brothers. (2 Corinthians 11:25–26)

Paul faced all of those things, yet he was not afraid to keep going. We can learn from Paul that even if we have been hurt physically, we don't have to allow the attack to traumatize us. If our personal safety is our goal, then any breach to the fortress we have built around us will create major panic. But if our goal, like Paul's, is to be about God's business, then we will realize that any attacks on our physical bodies are part of the battle we are in to advance God's purpose on earth. Like Paul, we will wear the scars of battle as a mark of a hero for Christ.

Satan has declared war on this planet, and we will experience casualties of war because we are under attack from him and his army. We need to accept the fact that we are in a war. Not accepting this will not make it go away; it will only make us unprepared for battle. God wants us to heed Peter's warning in 1 Peter 5:8, "Be self-controlled and alert. Your enemy the devil prowls around like a roaring lion looking for someone to devour," and Jesus' words in John 10:10, "The thief comes only to steal and kill and destroy; I have come that they may have life, and have it to the full." It is when we cling to Jesus and the life and power He offers that we will overcome our fears and have a full life.

Has someone stolen your innocence? Has someone or something tried to destroy you? Know that God has sent you a deliverer. No matter what someone has taken from you, know that God has the power to renew you with His life.

# How God Used
# My Pain for His Glory

Several years ago, we were in the midst of several big projects at Inspire Women when I came down with a horrible migraine. I had so much work to do, but the migraine was debilitating. I said to God, "I can't stay down, so please help me to get up. You didn't get off the cross even when Your head was throbbing from the thorns. You made up your mind to finish, and You were prepared to do whatever it took. I want to finish, too, God."

I knew my children were watching. I knew others were watching, too, to see what I would do. I knew that how I responded would affect how they would respond to suffering in their lives.

I had earlier thought it was bad timing for me to be struggling with physical pain during a time when there was so much work to be done in the ministry. But God told me that the timing of my physical problem was perfect to bring Him the most honor and glory. He used the migraine to remind me of the crown of thorns that Jesus wore on the cross, and He asked me to render my suffering as my form of worship. If I would serve Him while I was in pain, that would show the world exactly how important He is to me.

God does not waste our suffering. There are times we may endure for a long time and then there are sufferings God allows only for a season. I learned that what I need to do is say to God, "Let this suffering accomplish Your purpose." If I am going to suffer, then let it do in me what God wanted the suffering to do or else I will have suffered for no reason. If we are going to suffer anyway, let it at least be our form of worship unto a King who is worthy.

# Chapter 10

## *When You*

### FEAR
### FAILURE

"It is the Lord Christ
you are serving."

Colossians 3:24

There is nothing that will bring more fear and dread into a computer user's heart than a blank screen and the words "system failure." If you have seen those two words, you understand. If you haven't, you have probably still heard or felt them in other parts of your life and experienced the pain that failure brings.

It is no wonder that the thought of failure causes fear in today's society. There has perhaps been no time in the history of the world when there has been so much focus on success—success in school, in work, in your family, and even in the smaller details of life. When we think we're going to fail, we are afraid to ask for help, because that in itself is seen as a form of failure. When we have failed, we are afraid to tell others because of what they will think of us. Sometimes it seems as if there is no way to get past the fear of failure. The truth is that we will fail. It's built into our sinful natures. But we serve a God who never fails.

# We Live by the
# Power of Christ's Perfection

When I was in corporate America, my company's leaders would use fear as an incentive to get the young consultants to work hard. I had attended an orientation session with the top graduates from Harvard, Stanford, Cornell, and MIT, which meant I was surrounded by people who were used to succeeding. The pressure to perform and the pressure to outperform myself stressed me out. I couldn't understand why being successful was so important, yet I worked hard to achieve success in my work because I constantly feared failure.

But when God took over my life, something dramatic took place. I still worked hard, but not because I believed my human flesh could attain perfection. I worked hard as my humble act of service for a God who is perfect, knowing that He has already covered my imperfections. My freedom came from reading Romans 3:22–24: "This righteousness from God comes through faith in Jesus Christ to all who believe. There is no difference, for all have sinned and fall short of the glory of God, and are justified freely by his grace through the redemption that came by Christ Jesus." Did you hear that? We *all* sin. We *all* fall short of God's glory. These verses took me from the arrogance of thinking that I could do anything perfectly to realizing that only God is perfect. In fact, I learned that if I could accept my imperfections I could relax and not put unrealistic demands on myself.

Psalm 103:15–16 helped me to take myself less seriously. It reads, "As for man, his days are like grass, he flourishes like a flower of the field; the wind blows over it and it is gone, and its place remembers it no more." When I ask myself, "What will this matter a hundred years from now?" I find myself letting go of details that used to send me into a tailspin. The fact is that when I am gone, the world will remember me no more.

The only thing that matters is that I have done my best to leave God's fingerprints behind me.

One of the greatest truths that helped set me free is found in Romans 8:3–4:

> For what the law was powerless to do in that it was weakened by the sinful nature, God did by sending his own Son in the likeness of sinful man to be a sin offering. And so he condemned sin in sinful man, in order that the righteous requirements of the law might be fully met in us, who do not live according to the sinful nature but according to the Spirit.

What these verses teach us is that God's Son was the only one who was able to fulfill the perfect requirements of God's law. God is the only one who has succeeded in everything. Jesus lived a perfectly holy life and then went to the cross to pay the price for our imperfections. He then offers us the gift of forgiveness for those same imperfections. More than that, He gives us the opportunity to fully meet God's standards "according to the Spirit." We live the full requirements of God according to the Spirit by admitting that in our human flesh we cannot attain perfection. The only way we can be perfect is by simply receiving Christ's perfection. Then by faith, we allow God to live His perfect life through us.

So how do we live our lives by the power of Christ's perfection? First, we no longer try to be impressive. We acknowledge that we have missed the standard. We then accept the gift of Christ's perfection and know that He has all the answers. We ask God to show us His answers, and we get out of the way by not arguing with Him. Instead, we offer our lives as a living sacrifice and say to God, "All my energy belongs to You. All my creativity belongs to You. All my diligence belongs to You. Use them as You will, and direct me to solve this problem or reach this goal." Are you so focused on successfully completing your goals by your own power that you have overwhelmed yourself? Perhaps it's time to focus on the perfection of Christ and then trust Him to show you day by day how to reach His goals.

The key to releasing your fear of failure is to give God your life as an act of worship and let Him control the results. If you have given God your best, then rest in knowing that He is pleased with you. At the end of the day, He is the only person you work for. You exist to fulfill *His* purposes, not anyone else's. Colossians 3:23–24 teaches us, "Whatever you do, work at it with all your heart, as working for the Lord, not for men, since you know that you will receive an inheritance from the Lord as a reward. It is the Lord Christ you are serving."

## We Are Heavenly Citizens

One situation in our lives where our "failure" can cause fear is when we are unemployed. Whether we are unemployed by our own choice or by the choices of others, if we are used to making money to support our family, being without a job can easily trigger all sorts of fears for our family's well-being. But we may also feel fear because our sense of identity has been taken away and we no longer know who we are.

We live in a culture where our jobs and our titles often define us. Sometimes I wonder if God deliberately allows our job circumstances to rock our world so that we will stop relying on human made foundations. Do you fear severing ties with an organization or a ministry because you don't want to let go of your title or role? Do you fear not knowing what you're supposed to do with your time when you wake up every morning without a job?

There was a time when I was among the ranks of the unemployed. During that time, I thought it would be a good idea to get some training to prepare myself for a time when I might reenter the workforce, so I signed up for a class. During the class break, everyone else was busy calling their offices on their cell phones to check in. I had no one to call. I wandered around by myself, trying to look busy and needed. But the fact was that nobody called me because nobody needed me. I was disconnected from any purpose that would make a difference. It is a painful experience to think that your existence or lack of it will not make any difference. But what I totally missed was that God missed me. God had a plan for my life, and when I forgot who He was and what He wanted to accomplish on earth, I forgot who I was.

What I failed to realize at the time was that God Himself established my identity when I accepted the gift of His Son. I was walking around like a vagrant, when I had already executed a transaction that secured my future for eternity. Of all the contracts I have ever made in my life, that one transaction was the most important, and I had forgotten about it.

God reminded me of my divine transaction to show me that I was misguided to fixate on an earthly title, role, or any other identity that is defined by a company, a ministry, or another human being. God defined my identity through my acceptance of Jesus as my Savior. God granted me heavenly citizenship when I received the gift of His Son as the full payment for my sins. This acceptance gave me a place in God's spiritual family tree. This is an identity that will not only carry me through life, but also through eternity! It is an identity that no court of law or human decision can steal from me.

God reinforced my heavenly citizenship through a specific encounter with someone who recognized me as a heavenly citizen even when I had forgotten it. I was in a store, and a lady approached me. She was in tears. She said she recognized me from a Christian event I had attended. Her husband was dying of cancer, and she said her tears were tears of joy because she was sure God had sent me to her to encourage her. She asked me to pray for her, so right there in the checkout line, I prayed for her.

When I left that store, I heard God say, "You felt lost without a title. Didn't you know that a title would limit you?" God took me through that time of unemployment so I could learn that He gave me the only title that was needed. I don't need a company or anyone else to give me a title. I am the daughter of the King of Kings. I am on a divine mission, and as such, God reserves the right to send me wherever He wishes. My identity is in God's family tree, and my task is to represent the values of my royal family tree wherever I go.

## God Is More Powerful than the Odds

We serve a God who can do anything. He will never fail in His mission. It doesn't matter what obstacles are in the way or what the odds are, God can do whatever He wants to do in order to carry out His purposes.

When Moses led the children of Israel to the edge of the Promised Land, he sent scouts into the land to survey the territory. They returned with the following report. "We went into the land to which you sent us, and it does flow with milk and honey! Here is its fruit. But the people who live there are powerful, and the cities are fortified and very large. We even saw descendants of Anak there" (Numbers 13:27–28). The people of Israel were facing a situation where the odds were against them. God does not hide the facts. He shows us clearly how the odds are stacked neatly against us. He doesn't want warriors to enter a battle without realizing the challenge ahead. However, in spite of the facts and the seemingly insurmountable odds, when God says, "Go!" He means "Go!"

God had told the Israelites that He was giving them the land, yet the people let their fear overcome them. But Caleb was focused on God's promise. "Then Caleb silenced the people before Moses and said, 'We should go up and take possession of the land, for we can certainly do it'" (Numbers 13:30).

Are you staring at odds that are against you? Do you spend your time analyzing the odds instead of making sure of what God has told you to do and then doing it? Do you allow statistics to manage your life, or do you believe in the God who defies odds?

Caleb didn't care about the odds, because he was focused on God's promises. He knew they were at the edge of a huge blessing. He knew God wanted the children of Israel to claim the Promised Land, and he trusted God to help them do it. He realized that God would not have gone to all the trouble of getting them that far only to leave them on their own. It was time to move forward and take the land. But the rest of the people were afraid of the odds. So instead of remembering God's promise, they started to worry about what it would take to go forward. Numbers 13:31–33 tells us their fears:

> But the men who had gone up with him said, "We can't attack those people; they are stronger than we are." And they spread among the Israelites a bad report about the land they had explored. They said, "The land we explored devours those living in it. All the people we saw there are of great size. . . . We seemed like grasshoppers in our own eyes, and we looked the same to them."

Have you been dwelling on the facts to the point that their voice is louder than God's voice? Have you allowed the facts to cause you to abandon the mission God charged you with? That is what the Israelites did. They not only abandoned the mission, but they also complained loudly about their situation.

> That night all the people of the community raised their voices and wept aloud. All the Israelites grumbled against Moses and Aaron, and the whole assembly said to them, "If only we had died in Egypt! Or in this desert! Why is the Lord bringing us to this land only to let us fall by the

sword? Our wives and children will be taken as plunder. Wouldn't it be better for us to go back to Egypt?" And they said to each other, "We should choose a leader and go back to Egypt." (Numbers 14:1–4)

In God's Word, we see over and over again that if the journey does not require sacrifice or risk, everyone is happy to go along. But once the cost is higher than expected, don't be surprised when the followers accuse the leader. If you are a leader in this position, you can soften your own pain when you manage your expectations. God shows us through the story of Moses that when God tries to stretch the faith of the people, the pattern of those who are faithless is to accuse the leader. They did it time and again with Moses. It is human nature for our fear to drive us to blame someone else for our predicament. However, the leader is not the one who is stretching us—God is. If we are to blame anyone, we should blame God. The leader is simply under God's authority and he or she is also having his or her faith stretched.

If you are one of those leaders who is having her faith stretched while her followers are wanting to revolt, you need to settle your own fears before you can help the others. If you don't have faith to go forward, you can't encourage others to take a leap of faith. In Moses' story, Moses and a few other key leaders were able to stand strong in the midst of the crisis. Numbers 14:5–9 tells us:

Then Moses and Aaron fell facedown in front of the whole Israelite assembly gathered there. Joshua son of Nun and Caleb son of Jephunneh, who were among those who had explored the land, tore their clothes and said to the entire Israelite assembly, "The land we passed through and explored is exceedingly good. If the Lord is pleased with us, he will lead us into that land, a land flowing with milk and honey, and will give it to us. Only do not rebel against the

Lord. And do not be afraid of the people of the land, because we will swallow them up. Their protection is gone, but the Lord is with us. Do not be afraid of them."

In so many words, they were telling the people that the victory was not based on facts or analysis, but on this criterion: "If the Lord is pleased with us."

What causes the Lord to be pleased with us? It is not our performance, but our surrender and our faith. God wants to know, "Who are you afraid of? What are you afraid of? Are you more afraid of a person or your circumstances than you are afraid of My displeasure for not obeying and trusting Me?" When the odds are against you, know that God is not surprised. He intentionally allowed the odds because He wants a people who will live by faith. God will never eliminate the need for faith in your life. Once you understand God's patterns, you will know what to do, and you will know that God never fails.

## How God Overcame the Odds in My Life

When I start to feel overwhelmed by the odds, it helps to look not only to the stories of our faith heroes, but also to instances in my own life when God beat the odds. One of those times was when I had to go back to Hong Kong to be interviewed by the United States Immigration officials in order to renew my residency papers so I could stay in America.

As I prepared for this encounter, I knew there was a good chance they would decline my petition. My only grounds for immigration were based on my relation to my half-brother, who was an American citizen. But my brother was born in China during the war, and he didn't have a birth certificate to prove who his mother was. The immigration officials had told me that we could submit a blood sample from our mother to try to prove our relationship, but since she was dead, that wouldn't work. So I went into the interview knowing that my only chance to go back to America to live was my relationship with a brother that I couldn't prove was actually my brother.

Since you know that I now live in America, you know that God beat the odds—that He found a way to get me back to the United States. And the way He did it proves that He has a sense of humor. I had spent the last few years of my life in Mississippi, and as a person who absorbs my environment, I had begun to speak with the accent of people from Mississippi. Ten minutes into the interview, the immigration officer started laughing. He said, "I have been out of my country for ten years, and I never thought I would hear a Mississippi accent coming out of the mouth of a Chinese woman. You want to live in our country?" I said quietly, "Yes." He said, "Fine," and then he stamped my papers and told me the interview was over. When I left that office, I felt God's Spirit celebrating within me.

God showed me years ago that when there was something I needed to happen for His purposes to be carried out, He would open the door, no matter what the odds were. All those years ago when I faced the immigration officials, I didn't know that God had Inspire Women on my platter—but He did. For me to be the founder of a ministry that was to be birthed in Houston, Texas, I had to be able to live in the United States. So God made a way for that to happen. In climbing that hill with God, He was training me for the mountains to come. Since that time, I have seen God carry me through many situations where the odds were against me.

Are the odds against you? Then remember you serve a God who specializes in surmounting impossible odds. More than that, He specializes in designing a custom-tailored program that trains His vessels to fulfill His dreams, no matter the odds.

# Chapter 11

## *When You*

### FEAR LOSING A LOVED ONE

"Yet will I hope in him."

Job 13:15

Have you ever feared getting word that something terrible has happened to someone you love? Maybe your son or daughter is in the military and serving in a war zone. Or perhaps your husband's job puts him in danger on occasion. It could be that you just fear a freak accident happening to a family member or close friend. Or maybe you have already lost someone and you fear the pain, the grief, and what the future will hold for you without that person. It is common to have these fears on occasion, but we don't have to let them overwhelm us.

Life is unpredictable. We don't know what will happen tomorrow, and it's a fact that sometimes God allows bad things to happen to us and to our loved ones. So how do we get past the unpredictability? It boils down to trusting that God will always operate out of His character of goodness. We discussed this matter at length in chapter 3. We must believe that God is good through all of the circumstances of our lives. It is imperative that we let what He did for us on the cross be the final verdict for His goodness—not what is currently happening in our lives. The fact that God is good should alleviate our fears.

## "Yet Will I Hope in Him"

Let's take a look at one of our faith heroes who lost almost everyone he held dear—Job. God allowed Satan to test Job, even to the point of allowing him to kill Job's ten children. Just after Job learned that all of his livestock (more than ten thousand animals) had been killed or stolen, one of his servants came to him with the following report. "Your sons and daughters were feasting and drinking wine at the oldest brother's house, when suddenly a mighty wind swept in from the desert and struck the four corners of the house. It collapsed on them and they are dead" (Job 1:18–19). Can you imagine finding out that all of your children are dead? Perhaps you can. Maybe you've been there.

Like any parent who hears of the loss of a child, we can feel his grief as we read, "At this, Job got up and tore his robe and shaved his head" (Job 1:20). Such an expression of grief would be understandable, but what was unusual is what we see in the second half of that verse: "Then he fell to the ground in worship." What? Job immediately worshiped the God who allowed all ten of his children to die? Yes, in spite of these losses and many others, Job was able to say, "Though he slay me, yet will I hope in him" (Job 13:15). What kind of thinking is this? Not only did Job continue to praise God, but he also kept his hope in Him.

Have you ever found yourself negotiating with God? I have. In the past, I would say things like, "Oh God, if You keep this from happening, I'll do (fill in the blank)." I would think of all of the dreadful things that could happen to my family and me, and then I lived in a nightmare of constant worrying, hoping those things would never come to pass. I lived in the hypothetical world of what-ifs. What if my mother died? What if I lost my son? What if I lost my husband? The list could go on and on, but the point is that the hypothetical world can fill you with fear.

But the hypothetical world can also fill you with hope and purpose. Job faced every parent's nightmare, but he survived—and kept his faith intact. He didn't fear anything else that might come his way. If Job could handle that situation, then he could handle anything, and so can we. One thing that has helped me to overcome my fears of what might happen is to change all of those what-ifs to "even ifs." I think of the worst-case scenario and say to myself, "Even if that happens, I will still hope in the Lord."

As members of God's family tree, we need to pay attention to the biblical patterns of how life unfolds for those who are serving God. We can see a pattern of how those who walked in faith clung stubbornly to God because they trusted in His goodness. When you find yourself in a place where you feel you have no answers and you don't know what's up or what's down, then cling to what you know—that God is good and that He loves you.

God is eternal, and therefore He lives from eternity past to eternity future. As a result, He doesn't view life from our earthly time frame. Although God promises His protection, there are times when God allows our loved ones to enter eternity future as His way of protecting them. I often hear parents who have lost children say, "This is not right. Children are supposed to bury their parents. Parents are not supposed to be burying their children." But God never promised those things.

I ministered to a woman once who moved from Chicago to Houston to get away from the gangs. She enrolled her teenage son in a Christian school, and he regularly attended the youth group at their church. He was driving home after a youth meeting one night when he was killed in a car accident.

His mother was devastated. She couldn't understand why God didn't protect him, especially after she had removed him from the dangerous situation in Chicago. She asked me how she could fill the loneliness in her heart and get past the loss of her son.

In my desire to offer her words of comfort, I asked God to show me a verse or passage in the Bible that would help her deal with the loss of her child. God led me to John 3:16. "For God so loved the world that he gave his one and only Son . . ." Though we sometimes forget this fact, God Himself let go of a Son. He watched His Son die a horrible death. How did He do it? The first part of that verse tells us it was because He loved the world so much. God's emotion of love was greater than the sorrow of His loss. Therefore, to learn from God, we must also allow the emotion of love to be greater than our emotion of sorrow.

The Lord showed me that we can take our greatest loss and offer it to God as our greatest love offering. So we say, "Father, this child is my very life. I take my greatest treasure and I willingly give him up and lay him at Your feet. Thank You for allowing me the privilege of letting go of my greatest treasure and to give You a gift that cost me something." When we do this, we have allowed our love to be greater than our sorrow. And then peace descends because we have conformed to the image of the God who created us in His image.

## "Your Maker Is Your Husband"

A woman in my Sunday school class told me that she came home one day and found all her belongings packed up and left outside her house. After twenty-five years of marriage, her husband decided he did not love her and threw her out. Another woman shared how she tried to use her credit card at a store and found it had been canceled. She went to the bank and discovered that her husband had withdrawn all their money. She was in the middle of a divorce hearing and was up against her attorney husband, who fought to keep all their assets and leave her with as little as possible.

Are you facing a situation where the man who was once your best friend is now your worst enemy? Is your heart filled with fear over a divorce you don't want and didn't ask for? Do you feel you have lost your umbrella of protection?

Maybe you have lost a husband to death. This kind of loss is different than what comes from a divorce because it does not come with the emotional baggage of betrayal. However, it still carries with it the deep loss of the one who was your best friend, your confidant, and your protector.

Regardless of the manner by which you have lost a husband, who do you turn to as you face life as a newly single person after years of marriage? In Isaiah 54:4–5, God says, "Do not be afraid; you will not suffer shame. Do not fear disgrace; you will not be humiliated. You will forget the shame of your youth and remember no more the reproach of your widowhood. For your Maker is your husband—the Lord Almighty is his name—the Holy One of Israel is your Redeemer." In these verses God is not specifically addressing widowhood or divorce but is speaking of His restoration of a rebellious people. However, we still find that God describes Himself as our Maker and our husband. During a time of experiencing the fear that comes with losing a husband, how comforting it is to know that our Maker is our husband!

Notice the words that say, "The Lord Almighty is his name." If you are a widow, your name may feel strange because it came from your husband, who is no longer with you. If you are a divorcée, you may be resenting the spouse who not only ripped the ring off your finger, but who also no longer wants you to use his name. At a time when you're not sure what your name is anymore, take comfort from the fact that your Maker and husband has a name, and He is called the Lord Almighty. Would you exchange the name you had with an earthly husband with that of being a wife who belongs to the Lord Almighty?

More than that, this husband is also the "Holy One of Israel." So often in a divorce, the other side makes up lies in an attempt to win their case. There is little honesty in a spouse who doesn't want you to have any of the assets you accumulated together. But the Lord Almighty is honest and is filled with integrity. You can trust His character. At a time when you don't know who you can trust, know that you can trust God.

The Lord Almighty is also "your Redeemer." If you have lost a spouse, do you find yourself regretting the things you wish you had said or done when he was alive? Were there trips you wish you had taken, and now it's too late? In the case of a divorce, no matter how right you may feel you are, any time there is a conflict there are two sides to the story. No matter how little you are at fault, something in you dies when you feel like such a failure. We need a redeemer who will cover us with His grace. We need a redeemer who will heal our heart and restore us with His mercy. We need a redeemer who is the creator of second chances and new beginnings.

## Carol's Story

A friend of mine who suffered through a terrible divorce has been single now for many years. She told me that at first, she was fearful of being alone, but now she is filled with hope. I would like to share her story with you, as I feel it will also bring hope to other women who have lost a spouse. Here is Carol's story in her own words.

*When my divorce was finally over I felt like I had come out of a battle zone and was so relieved that I had survived. As much as I felt that I would rather be alone than be miserably married, I still had to adjust to the fact that I was on my own. I was facing things like Valentine's Day without a*

*Valentine, Thanksgiving dinner without the usual family, and my birthday without the person who once was my counterpart. The aloneness was most vivid when I was ill and there was no one to drive me to the doctor or when the car broke down and I felt stranded. It was during these times that I cried out to God to be my husband.*

*Right after Hurricane Katrina, there was a major storm heading for Houston. Everyone was leaving town. I was terrified because I knew I could not drive myself. I felt so utterly alone and trapped while waiting for the hurricane to hit. I asked the Lord to help me. A friend who lived in Dallas offered to fly to Houston to drive me to her home in Dallas. Never in a million years would I have expected anyone to reach out to me that way. Once again, God showed me that even before we cry out to Him, He already has the answers.*

*I own a small building that I lease out to a company. One day, the company called to say a garbage truck had hit the fence while picking up the garbage and the fence could not close anymore. I called the garbage company and they said they would take a look at the problem the next day, but no one came. So I prayed, "Father, You know I don't have the money to replace this fence. I pray that the garbage company will fix it." The next morning I got a phone call telling me the fence was fixed. The garbage company had fixed it the night before. The Lord had answered my prayer while I slept.*

*While on my own, I had been praying for quite a while that the Lord would give me a worldwide ministry—one that would count for Him for all eternity. A number of months later I was bedridden because of my heart. I asked the Lord if I could do a ministry while in bed. A few days later Anita Carman called me and asked me to be her prayer warrior. I said, "Yes!" because I knew this was God's answer to my prayers. Not only did the Lord answer my prayer while I was in bed, but Inspire Women is beginning to go nationwide and will eventually go worldwide! God showed me that as long as*

*He is in my life, we will be conquering the world together. It has been my utmost privilege to stay on my knees on behalf of Inspire Women. I have watched the ministry soar. Every time I hear of the doors God has opened, I say, "Thank You, Father. I knew You would do it!"*

*Paul said in 1 Corinthians 7:34, "An unmarried woman or virgin is concerned about the Lord's affairs: Her aim is to be devoted to the Lord in both body and spirit." God has been my husband, and my life has been an adventure. I praise God for the women who have found an earthly counterpart to walk with them through life. But for those who are single, I want you to know that being single is not a liability or some inferior state you feel you are settling for as if life is better elsewhere. It is a different calling whether for a season or for a lifetime. And with all of God's callings, it is perfect because it was designed by a good God who loves us with all His heart.*

## How God Helped Me Overcome My Fear of Loss

If you have children, you have most likely known the fear of losing them. There has probably been a situation where you feared for their lives. I have known this fear.

When my boys were in elementary school, I decided it would be a good idea for the family to go to the Schlitterbahn Water Park. This was not just your run-of-the-mill water park, but a sixty-five-acre resort filled with numerous pools, waterslides, tubing rivers, water coasters, and so on. While we were there, my six- and eight-year-old boys decided they wanted to go down a huge waterslide that emptied into a large pool nearby. I told them to go ahead and that I would wait for them by the pool.

I waited and waited. They didn't come. I finally sent my husband up the four flights of stairs to the top of the slide to see if they were there. They were not. And he discovered that those stairs led to a slide that emptied into a pool on the other side of the park—a forty-five-minute walk away. Panic shot through me. "Go after them!" I cried out to my husband.

As I sat there by the pool, I started imagining all sorts of scenarios. I wondered if the park would close down. I imagined looking for bodies. I thought about how my younger son couldn't swim very well. The day had definitely not ended up being the wonderful family day I had expected.

And still I waited. Finally, I saw my husband walking back toward me . . . with no boys. He said he found the end of the slide and they were nowhere to be seen. His next mission was to file a missing children report with the park. So I waited some more. While I sat there, I said, "Lord, You can see them. You know where they are." I reminded God of how when I told my older son the story of Cain and Abel, I had explained to him, "The moral of the story is that you are your brother's keeper." As I sat there worrying about where they were, I asked God to help him remember that.

Another twenty minutes went by. Then off in the distance, I saw them. My two boys were shuffling toward me, dragging big rubber tubes behind them. I said to them calmly, "Come here, sit down, and tell me all about it." My older son explained what had happened. "When I saw we would let out at the other end of the park, I knew you'd be worried, and I knew we had to stick together. Then halfway down the slide, it split in two directions. Thomas's tube started going down one side, and mine was going the other way. I paddled as fast as I could and grabbed onto his tube so we could go down together on the same side. The whole time, all I could hear in my head was, 'You are your brother's keeper! You are your brother's keeper!'"

The first verse my son learned in Sunday school was this one: "I have hidden your word in my heart that I might not sin against you" (Psalm 119:11). I know God does not guarantee us safety in this world, but I praise Him for the times He protected my children by bringing His Word to their remembrance. And I also praise Him for the times His Word has carried me through my fears and losses. In His Word I have found counsel for all situations in my life.

# Chapter 12

## *When You*

### ARE AFFECTED BY THE CHOICES OF OTHERS

"I will be joyful in God my Savior."

Habakkuk 3:18

*Y*our coworker tells lies about you and you get fired as a result. Someone runs a red light and you end up in the hospital. A generous donor tells you he can no longer be so generous. Your sixteen-year-old daughter tells you she's pregnant. An employee or team member quits in the middle of a major project.

In what ways have you been affected by the choices of others—affected by things you can't control? It's not a matter of *if* other people's choices will make an impact on your world in a major way, it's a matter of *when*. Though we wish it were different, God does allow us to suffer or to be greatly inconvenienced by decisions that we have no control over. Yet we don't have to let those decisions control our emotions or our future.

## Roll with the Changes

As we have looked at the stories of our faith heroes to discover the royal family's code of conduct, we have often turned to the life of Moses. And once again, his experiences fit in with the topic at hand. There were many times that the choices other people made greatly affected Moses' life. But the incident that had the most long-lasting effect was when the Israelites refused to enter the Promised Land and were therefore relegated to wander in the wilderness for forty years while most of them died. In that situation, there were a few who were willing to obey God's command to take possession of the land—Moses, Caleb, and Joshua—but since the others refused to be obedient to God, those three also had to suffer the consequences. They, too, had to ramble through that desert, living in tents and eating manna for forty years.

Things are no different today than they were back then. We still have to pay the price for other people's decisions—and they sometimes have to pay the price for our decisions, as well. It's also important to note that those decisions aren't always a result of disobedience. Sometimes the decisions we make in order to carry out God's mission for our lives can have a big effect on others, and vice versa. But then there are the times when the decision was simply sinful. That was the case with the Israelites.

Moses' mission was sabotaged by the very people he was trying to bless . . . the people *God* was trying to bless. After all they had been through, and after all Moses had done to get them there, the Israelites rebelled against him and, more importantly, against God and they refused to enter the Promised Land.

We know that God was not pleased with them. He said,

> As surely as I live and as surely as the glory of the Lord fills the whole earth, not one of the men who saw my glory and the miraculous signs I performed in Egypt and in the desert but who disobeyed me and tested me ten times—not one of them will ever see the land I promised on oath to their forefathers. No one who has treated me with contempt will ever see it. (Numbers 14:21–23)

The people who disobeyed God faced very dire consequences. But don't miss the fact that God's judgment affected innocent people too. While God didn't condemn Moses, Joshua, and Caleb to death in the wilderness along with the rest of the Israelites, He did condemn them to many long years of waiting—years they thought would be spent in the Promised Land. God's judgment also affected the children (both born and unborn) of those who were disobedient. Undoubtedly, some of them died during those forty years, and others had to move from place to place throughout the desert for most of their lifetimes because of the choices their parents made.

The consequences of wrong choices other people make may change your world, alter your schedule, and otherwise make a huge impact on the rest of your life. God reserves the right to protect you, but He also has the liberty to allow the bad choices of others to affect your entire life in major ways. Your innocence will not save you from the choices of others. So how do you combat the fear that comes from dealing with those situations? You need to settle in your heart that even with those consequences you must face, God still has a plan.

Do you think God didn't know that His people would refuse to go into the Promised Land? Of course He knew, and of course He still had a plan for them and for Moses. And He still has a plan for you, even when you're facing uncertainties. In our minds we might call it Plan B. However, we know that God is sovereign and that in His mind, it's actually Plan A, because He knew what was going to happen all along. Whatever happens was part of His original plan. But for us, when Plan A goes awry, we need to turn to what we call Plan B.

Are you looking at a Plan B? Even when it seems as if your plans have fallen apart, you still have a mission. You still have an end goal, and God will help you accomplish it. Moses did not abandon his mission. He kept leading that obstinate group of people, because that's what God had told him to do. Though the timeline had extended, the mission stayed the same. Moses flowed with the changes and continued the mission the best way he knew how. The people had made a wrong choice, but Moses made the right choice by sticking with God's mission, no matter what the consequences were. In the same way, when life throws a curve ball your way, follow the example of our faith hero Moses and keep making the right choices. We can't control what other people do, but we can control what we do. We can choose to be obedient.

While we do take our cues for royal behavior from our faith heroes in the Bible, we must also understand that, with the exception of Jesus, they were sinful humans, too. Moses didn't always do the right thing. He wasn't always obedient. In fact, he missed out on entering the Promised Land because he struck out in anger against the Israelites. He looked away from the mission for a moment and he let his anger and irritation with the people disqualify him from receiving God's blessing. My prayer is that we won't let that happen to us.

I have found that the times I become afraid are the times when I compare my expectations of how I want life to be to what is required of me under the new direction God's plan is taking. When I look at how long something will take under this new plan, it overwhelms me when there is something else I want to do or think I should be doing with that time. When I see how much money it will take to counteract the consequences of another person's choice, I get resentful if there was something else I wanted to do with that money. I get scared about what I stand to lose by following the new plan, and I don't want to do it. But when I realize that I exist for God's purpose and that He owns everything—including my time—then I can be free from fear. I can say, "God, do whatever it takes, but I can only give what I have. So if You want it, take it all." When I no longer own my time, my energy, or my resources, then all I need to do is to be obedient to walk through whatever open door is there to continue with the original mission. I find freedom in my obedience, and so can you.

# Beware of Angry People

We know that we can't control other people's actions, but we also need to realize that we can't control their emotions, either. The emotion in others that is most likely to cause fear in us and to lead the other person to make bad choices in relation to us is anger. There are times when fear is warranted. In fact, a healthy fear is one of God's ways to protect us from evil. When we fear angry people, it will cause us to avoid them, which in turn protects us.

The first mention of human anger in the Bible is in the story of Cain and Abel. As is often the case, Cain's anger was evoked because of his jealousy of his brother Abel.

> The Lord looked with favor on Abel and his offering, but on Cain and his offering he did not look with favor. So Cain was very angry, and his face was downcast. Then the Lord said to Cain, "Why are you angry? Why is your face downcast? If you do what is right, will you not be accepted? But if you do not do what is right, sin is crouching at your door; it desires to have you, but you must master it." Now Cain said to his brother Abel, "Let's go out to the field." And while they were in the field, Cain attacked his brother Abel and killed him. (Genesis 4:4–8)

Cain was angry because God favored Abel. God gave Cain the opportunity to do what was right to also gain His favor, but he chose not to. Instead, he chose to lash out in anger, and his choice gravely affected Abel's life. Since you are reading this book, you have obviously never had anyone make the drastic choice to kill you. But have you ever experienced the wrath of someone who blamed you for his or her failure? Instead of recognizing our own mistakes, as sinful people we often choose to strike out at the objects of our resentment.

We should have a healthy fear of those who are angry,

because their anger could lead to our harm—whether it's emotional or physical. It would be foolish to ignore the fact that someone is angry with you. God's Word shows us time and time again that often it's only a matter of time before those who are angry with us will strike out at us.

To illustrate this, let's take a look at another story we're already familiar with—that of David and Saul. David entered Saul's court to soothe him with harp music. He protected Saul by risking his life to face Goliath. He fought battles under Saul's authority. Saul should have been happy with all of David's service, yet he ended up being jealous of David's success and popularity. And his jealousy led to anger. First Samuel 18:8–9 tells us, "Saul was very angry . . . 'They have credited David with tens of thousands,' he thought, 'but me with only thousands. What more can he get but the kingdom?' And from that time on Saul kept a jealous eye on David." God's Word specifically referred to Saul as having a "jealous eye" toward David. Have you ever had someone watch your every move because they were worried you might get ahead of them in accomplishments? Has that led you to fear them? Has their anger toward you altered your life?

Proverbs 29:22 warns us, "An angry man stirs up dissension, and a hot-tempered one commits many sins." It is dangerous to try to reason with an angry person, because that person is bound to commit sins in their anger. They will allow the waves of anger inside them to spill over on those around them. Angry people do not operate out of logic but out of emotion.

We know that David tried to reconcile with Saul many times, but after each time, Saul again became angry and jealous. He became angry to the point that he was on a mission to kill David. So for years David had to run from Saul. Because of Saul's choice to let his anger and jealousy rule over him, David paid the price of having to spend a whole season of his life away from his family, his friends, and his home. Yet he refused to let anger rule over him and he didn't kill Saul when he had the chance. David stayed obedient to God.

## Stick with the Mission

Often when someone makes a choice that negatively affects your life, it's someone you're not that close to, someone you don't especially like, or perhaps even someone you don't know. But what about when it's someone you love? What about those times when someone who promised to be there for you, your business, or your ministry chooses to break that promise?

During one of Jesus' most vulnerable times in His journey on earth, the very disciple who promised to never abandon Him broke that promise. We, too, may someday find ourselves in a situation where the person who was closest to us will end up abandoning us in our greatest time of need.

Peter was one of Jesus' best friends; he was part of the inner circle with James and John. He thought he could—and would—stick with Jesus through anything. In fact, after Jesus told His disciples that they would all fall away from Him, Peter responded, "Even if all fall away, I will not" (Mark 14:29). Jesus knew that Peter would break that promise. But we also know that the preknowledge of Peter's abandonment didn't make Jesus turn back from what He knew He was about to face.

Jesus knew that all of his disciples would abandon Him. Yet He also knew He wouldn't be alone. He said in John 16:32, "But a time is coming, and has come, when you will be scattered, each to his own home. You will leave me all alone. Yet I am not alone, for my Father is with me." He did not let the abandonment and broken promises of His disciples discourage Him from doing what had to be done—dying on the cross. He stuck with His mission to the end, despite the bad choices of others.

In Jesus' example, we find the power to keep going until

we have finished the work God trusted us to do. For all the examples of those who have or will break their promises to us, we serve a God who stayed with us to the end. We have Jesus' example of sticking to the mission until His work was done. Why did He stay? Why did He not turn back when everyone had left Him? He stayed because of us. He said, "Father, I want those you have given me to be with me where I am, and to see my glory, the glory you have given me because you loved me before the creation of the world" (John 17:24). Jesus knew that the only way for us to be with Him was to finish the work on the cross. We, also, should stay with our mission because of what is at stake. Our tenacity to finish the work God gave us to do will come when we make the connection that our activities affect the lives of others for eternity. No other cause is worthy of pouring out your life.

## God Will Restore Us

When we are filled with fear over the consequences we face due to other people's decisions, we should refocus on the promise of all promises. After Adam and Eve sinned in the Garden of Eden, even as God voiced His judgment upon them and Satan, He made a promise to send a seed from woman to crush the devil (Genesis 3:15). When Jesus came into the world and died on the cross for us, He paid the full penalty of the sins of the world and crushed Satan's plan to rob God of His children. We can find our confidence in the fulfillment of God's promise to offer fallen humanity a plan of restoration.

Since God has restored the greatest loss on planet Earth—the loss of perfection, of sinlessness—then surely He can restore the small losses in our lives. It is with this confidence that we can say, "Even if someone makes a decision that changes the course of my life, I believe God has another plan." God is the master planner, and He can redeem and restore any situation.

We alleviate our fears when we no longer have to trust in the promises and choices of fallen humanity. We find our true security when we trust the promises of our heavenly Father. The prophet Habakkuk expressed his trust in God in this way: "Though the fig tree does not bud and there are no grapes on the vines, though the olive crop fails and the fields produce no food, though there are no sheep in the pen and no cattle in the stalls, yet I will rejoice in the Lord, I will be joyful in God my Savior" (Habakkuk 3:17–18). God restores the joy in our hearts no matter how our circumstances appear, because we have the confidence that God will always come through for those who trust Him.

## How God Uses My Fears to Reveal His Power

As God led me into ministry, I realized that there were some wounds in my life that He did not deliberately take away. I found that certain events or situations would open up the wounds from my past—the results of choices that other people made that I could not control. I asked God to take away those memories and eradicate parts of my history from my mind, but He chose not to. For example, one of my biggest challenges in ministry is to trust those who make promises to me. Trust is difficult for me, perhaps because of the betrayal I felt from my mother.

For so many years as I was growing up, my mother and I dreamed of coming to America together. No matter what challenges came along, we promised we would always be there for each other and together we would make it. Then when I woke up one morning at the age of seventeen to find that she had taken her own life, my whole world unraveled. I saw her exit as the greatest act of betrayal because she had promised to be there for me, but then she left me to continue the journey alone. Logically, I can argue that she was in a lot of despair and that her suicide had nothing to do with me. But emotionally, her act made me afraid to ever depend on anyone on any significant journey in my life.

I carried that emotional baggage with me as God entrusted me with His work. But in ministry, much of the work requires teaming up with others and rallying the body of Christ. God's heart is for the world, so He is not interested in us taking solo journeys with Him. He wants us to be in community, and He wants His leaders to bring their communities along on the mission He has given them. So my emotional challenge arises when someone I depended on makes me a promise and then breaks it.

In my early days in ministry, I was unsure of my calling and depended on the affirmation of key individuals. One such individual encouraged me to take a step of faith in establishing Inspire Women. She assured me she would always be there for me. Then after I had cut the umbilical cord to an established organization and was on my own in creating a new ministry, she severed her support because she was drawn away by other interests. Her lack of support opened up the wounds from my past. I found myself crying out the same way I had when my mother exited from my life, "You said you would never leave me, but you left!" God had to show me that as the royal daughter of a King and one trusted with God's mission, I must stop operating out of the child in me. What happened in my childhood belongs to the past. How many more days will I allow my past to cripple me when God desires to transform my emotions for His future?

God healed my heart by telling me, "In your relationships, there may be things you feel you need as a daughter, a wife, or a mother, but I am inviting you to operate as My ambassador. In that role, you set aside your needs as daughter, mother, and wife, and step into your calling as an ambassador of Jesus Christ. Your emotional need does not give you an excuse to compromise My calling in your life." I learned that God's power is there to overcome what is emotionally missing in my personal life. The devil's lie is that certain events or relationships will paralyze us. God's truth is that those He calls, He will empower.

Today, when I look back at the incidents in my life where people broke their promises or made other choices that caused me suffering, I realized God allowed them in my path to show me His power to overcome my past and my fears. If God hasn't removed your wounds, it was meant to remind you that whenever the need arises, His power will be there to overcome the wounds and fears and will keep you going. God is not afraid of your past. You shouldn't be, either.

# Afterword

As I was writing in my study one day, my husband quietly entered the room and just stood there. I looked up to see if he had something to tell me. He hesitated before saying, "Yogi died." Yogi was our fifteen-year-old French sheepdog whose vision had grown worse over the years and whose legs collapsed out from under him every other day, but who somehow always bounced back up and kept going. He loved running in the sun, devouring his dog biscuits, and simply celebrating being alive. We had been sure he would outlive us all. In fact, I had heard Yogi that very morning, barking nonstop at the wind, still proud of his role as watchdog. "What do you mean?" I asked. My husband replied, "He's not moving. I think he's dead."

I went to check on Yogi, and sure enough, there was no life in him. He must have slipped away during his morning nap. As my husband made arrangements with the local SPCA to take care of the body, I reflected on our time with Yogi. I thought about how quickly the years had flown by and how precious each moment is.

How much time will we have before there will be no more life in us? In the time that we have, are we soaring freely the way God intended, or are we living in bondage to situations that break our heart and keep us prisoners to our own emotions?

As we conclude this time in our journey together, my prayer for you is that you will walk into your future as a woman who is free from bondage to the sin and emotions that have kept you from fulfilling God's purpose for your life. Take a look at the overarching principles of this book one more time.

1. As believers, we are members of God's royal family.
2. Our royal family has royal customs that are part of our heritage and identity.
3. We reinforce our royal identity by continuously acting as a member of God's family ought to.
4. The customs of God's royal family are concretely stated in the Bible. We are to follow these instructions.
5. If a verse does not speak to our situation, we are to study the lives of the faith heroes in God's Word and learn how to respond from their parallel experiences.

My hope is that you will assimilate those principles into the way you live for the rest of your life. Transforming our emotions for God's purposes can only bring us greater joy and fulfillment.

I would like to share one final incident from my life where I used the principles above in response to a situation that crushed my heart to the point that I almost abandoned God's dream. The situation involved a large amount of disillusionment with a leader I had esteemed highly. I was broken-hearted as I observed how a friend who had begun so purely started to make decisions that were self-serving.

As soon as I felt the stabs in my heart that resulted from this situation, I ran to God for counsel. I desperately searched for something in God's Word that would guide me. I wasn't satisfied with just the general guidance of forgiveness and the overall concept of trusting God. I needed something more concrete that I could sink my teeth into, so I asked God to show me a parallel situation to my own in the Bible.

In response to my confusion about how someone who began so well could end so tragically, God led me to the story of Moses. The story is told in Numbers 20:2–12, and it reads as follows:

> Now there was no water for the community, and the people gathered in opposition to Moses and Aaron. They quarreled with Moses and said, "If only we had died when our brothers fell dead before the Lord! Why did you bring the Lord's community into this desert, that we and our livestock should die here? Why did you bring us up out of Egypt to this terrible place? It has no grain or figs, grapevines or pomegranates. And there is no water to drink!" Moses and Aaron went from the assembly to the entrance to the Tent of Meeting and fell facedown, and the glory of the Lord appeared to them. The Lord said to Moses, "Take the staff, and you and your brother Aaron gather the assembly together. Speak to that rock before their eyes and it will pour out its water. You will bring water out of the rock for the community so they and their livestock can drink." So Moses took the staff from the Lord's presence, just as he commanded him. He and Aaron gathered the assembly together in front of the rock and Moses said to them, "Listen, you rebels, must we bring you water out of this rock?" Then Moses raised his arm and struck the rock twice with his staff. Water gushed out, and the community and their livestock drank. But the Lord said to Moses and Aaron, "Because you did not trust in me enough to honor me as holy in the sight of the Israelites, you will not bring this community into the land I give them."

What God led me to do as a result of reading this story was to focus on Moses' emotions. I asked myself what emotion he was repressing that eventually erupted in sin. I looked back at the passage and noticed that Moses called the Israelites "rebels." And in his words, "Must we bring you water out of this rock?" we can hear his resentment. The sentiment of this question was, "What else do you want from me after all my years of serving you?"

Moses was a leader who had served for years. He had put up with a faithless group and suffered the consequence of wandering in the desert for forty years because of their choices. Through it all, Moses had been faithful, but he eventually let his emotions overcome him, and he missed out on entering the Promised Land because of it.

We, too, can find that after pouring out and pouring out, we end up irritated with the very people God trusts us to lead. Instead of serving them, we find ourselves criticizing them, being angry with them, calling them names, talking about them behind their backs, and a host of other hurtful things, instead of praying for them. There is much danger in experiencing emotional burnout, feeling fed up, and being ready to get a project over with so we can just be done with the people involved.

In Moses' story, I saw how his frame of mind paralleled the leader in my life that I had so admired. This leader had grown irritated because of all the years of service in the midst of those who had delayed the work because of their faithlessness. The leader no longer wanted to trust God for the strength to lead, but instead had gone down the path of entitlement. The resulting attitude was one of, "After all I've done for you, what else do you want from me? I'll help because it might be the politically correct thing to do or because circumstances force me to, but my heart is not in it. And you can be sure that when no one else is looking, I will not make one decision that will help you! It's payback time. It's time for you to bless me, not for me to bless you!"

My heart was broken to see what had happened to Moses and to my leader. At the same time, God healed my heart with Moses' story because I saw the warning for my own life. I will spend many years building Inspire Women. I will have both victories and setbacks. I will experience delays caused by the faithless decisions of those around me. The acts of others will cost me time and energy, and they will require longer hours and more sacrifice for me and for the ministry's staff. I will grieve to see how those who didn't trust God will lose the blessing God intended for them. But through this journey, what God wants to know is how I will respond at the end. Will I become irritated or resentful? Will I feel like someone owes me? Will I manipulate things because of what I think I deserve?

Through reading and understanding Moses' story, I was able to overcome my disillusionment with a leader by learning how vulnerable leaders are as they enter the final season of their service. If someone like Moses could have fallen, then how much more could any other leader fall into the same temptation? This story helped me to pray for those who were deceived at the end. It also helped me to focus on my own walk and to ask God to keep me from being deceived.

As I have said before, faith is not a mystical experience, but the concrete application of God's Word in our lives. We are royalty, and royalty has a royal code of behavior. We can let our emotions control us or we can submit our emotions to the customs of God's royal family. We need to let God examine what we are feeling, and then we should invite Him to use His Word to show us how we should respond to our situations. We learn from the right things our faith heroes did, as well as from their mistakes.

I pray this book encouraged you in a special way. Know that I believe in your victory song because I believe in the power of God's Word released in you as you put His Word into action.

# LEADING WOMEN WHO WOUND

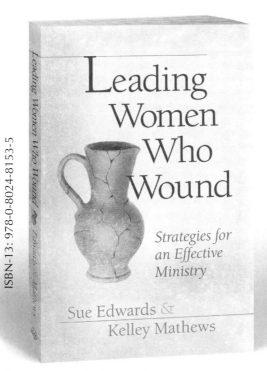

Given the fallen nature of the human heart as well as the complexities of personalities, conflict is an inevitable aspect of ministry. How do women deal with emotions when other women are insensitive, manipulative, or just plain mean? Seasoned women's ministry leaders themselves, Sue Edwards and Kelley Mathews walk through several different aspects of conflict resolution including self-examination, identification of potential sources of conflict, tools for conflict resolution, and insight on how to prevent and move beyond conflict in order to move forward with integrity.

1-800-678-8812 • MOODYPUBLISHERS.COM

# DISCERNING THE VOICE OF GOD

ISBN-13: 978-0-8024-5279-5

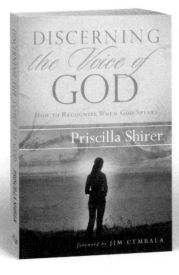

"Recognizing God's voice is not just a privilege given to a select few. It is the right of every believer." By studying the Word of God and heightening our spiritual senses to hear the still small voice of God, women can indeed recognize the promptings of the Holy Spirit. From the Old Testament prophets to modern day believers, Priscilla walks the reader through Scripture that captures the method and tone of God's communication and teaches the reader to beware of counterfeit voices. How we each encounter God's voice may differ, but the nature of it does not.

# HE SPEAKS TO ME

ISBN-13: 978-0-8024-5007-4

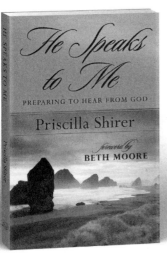

God has a message for you! Do you want to develop a more intimate prayer life? Even more, do you want to hear from God in practical ways? Let Priscilla Shirer prepare you by giving you a deeper understanding of the Holy Spirit. Based on the life of Samuel, who first heard God's voice while still a small boy, and packed with practical examples from Priscilla's own life, *He Speaks to Me* speaks directly to the need to develop a richer prayer life and a deeper, more intimate relationship with God.

1-800-678-8812 • MOODYPUBLISHERS.COM

# The Silent Seduction of Self-Talk

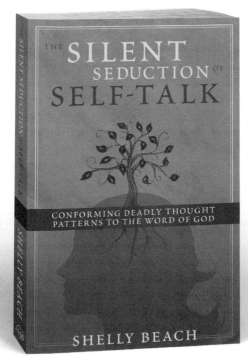

We speak to ourselves at a rate of 1,300 words per minute, making constant assessments and judgments often filtered through sinful and selfish agendas. These dialogues can make us blind to the scriptural truth that the vision we hold of ourselves and the reality of our walk in Christ are often polar opposites. Shelly provides practical tools that help readers surface the inner conflicts that churn below the waterline of their awareness. She explores real-life examples and includes tools to assist in the spiritual disciplines of self-assessment, repentance, commitment, and transformation.

1-800-678-8812 • MOODYPUBLISHERS.COM